where we stand

where we stand:

CLASS MATTERS

bell hooks

ROUTLEDGE
NEW YORK AND LONDON

Published in 2000 by
Routledge
29 West 35th Street
New York, NY 10001

Published in Great Britain by
Routledge
11 New Fetter Lane
London EC4P 4EE

Routledge is an imprint of the Taylor & Francis Group
Copyright © 2000 by Gloria Watkins

Printed in the United States of America on acid free paper.

Library of Congress Cataloging-in-Publication Data

hooks, bell
    where we stand : class matters / bell hooks.
        p. cm.
    Includes index.
    ISBN 0-415-92911-3 — ISBN 0-415-92913-X (pbk.)
        1. Social classes—United States. 2. United States—Race relations. I. Title.

HN90.S6 H66 2000
305.5'0973—dc21   00-034470

contents

where we stand

Nowadays it is fashionable to talk about race or gender; the uncool subject is class. It's the subject that makes us all tense, nervous, uncertain about where we stand. In less than twenty years our nation has become a place where the rich truly rule. At one time wealth afforded prestige and power, but the wealthy alone did not determine our nation's values. While greed has always been a part of American capitalism, it is only recently that it has set the standard for how we live and interact in everyday life.

Many citizens of this nation, myself included, have been and are afraid to think about class. Affluent liberals concerned with the plight of the poor and dispossessed are daily mocked and ridiculed. They are blamed for all the problems of the welfare state. Caring and sharing have come to be seen as traits of the idealistic weak. Our nation is fast becoming a class-segregated society where the plight of the poor is forgotten and the greed of the rich is morally tolerated and condoned.

As a nation we are afraid to have a dialogue about class even though the ever-widening gap between rich and poor has already set the stage for ongoing and sustained class warfare. As a citizen who moved from the working class to a world of affluence I have long struggled to make sense of class in my life, to come to terms with what it means to have a lot when many people have so little. In my case, among those who have so little are my own family and friends. Like a vast majority of women in this nation I believe in caring and sharing. I want to live in a world where there is enough of everything basic and necessary to go around. Applying these beliefs to everyday life experience has not been an easy or simple matter.

These essays on class address the issues of both national and personal responsibility. I write about the class issues that most intimately affect my life and the lives of many other folks who are trying to figure out how to be responsible, who believe in justice, who want to take a stand. I write personally about my journey from a working-class world to class consciousness, about how classism has undermined feminism, about solidarity with the poor and how we see the rich. Of course, these essays address consumerism and the ways lust for affluence creates a politics of greed.

Women of all races and black men are rapidly becoming the poorest of the poor. Breaking the silence—talking about class and coming to terms with where we stand—is a necessary step if we are to live in a world where prosperity and plenty can be shared, where justice can be realized in our public and private lives. The time to talk about class, to know where we stand, is now—before it is too late, before we are all trapped in place and unable to change our class or our nation's fate.

bell hooks

Class Matters

Everywhere we turn in our daily lives in this nation we are confronted with the widening gap between rich and poor. Whether it is the homeless person we walk by as we go about daily chores in urban areas, the beggars whose cups tinkle with the sound of a few coins, the middle-class family member or friend who faces unemployment due to cutbacks, plant closings, or relocation, or the increased cost of food and housing, we are all aware of class. Yet there is no organized class struggle, no daily in-your-face critique of capitalist greed that stimulates thought and action—critique, reform, and revolution.

As a nation we have become passive, refusing to act responsibly toward the more than thirty-eight million citizens who live in poverty here and the working masses who labor long and hard but still have difficulty making ends meet. The rich are getting richer. And the poor are falling by the wayside. At times it seems no one cares. Citizens in the middle who live comfortable lives, luxurious lives in relation to the rest of the world, often fear that challenging classism will be their downfall, that simply by expressing concern for the poor they will end up like them, lacking the basic necessities of life. Defensively, they turn their backs on the poor and look to the rich for answers, convinced that the good life can exist only when there is material affluence.

More and more, our nation is becoming class-segregated. The poor live with and among the poor—confined in gated communities without adequate shelter, food, or health care—the victims of predatory greed. More and more poor communities all over the country look like war zones, with boarded-up bombed-out buildings, with either the evidence of gunfire everywhere or the vacant silence of unsatisfied hunger. In some neighborhoods, residents must wear name tags to gain entrance to housing projects, gated camps that are property of the nation-state. No one safeguards the interests of citizens there; they are soon to be the victims of class genocide. This is the passive way our country confronts the poor and indigent, leaving them to die from street warfare, sugar, alcohol, and drug addiction, AIDS, and/or starvation.

The rich, along with their upper-class neighbors, also live in gated communities where they zealously protect their class interests—their way of life—by surveillance, by security forces, by direct links to the police, so that all danger can be kept at bay. Strangers entering these neighborhoods who look like they do not belong, meaning that they are the wrong color and/or have the appearance of being lower class, are stopped and vetted. In my affluent neighborhood in Greenwich Village, I am often stopped by shopkeepers and asked where I work, whose children do I keep, the message being you must not live here—you do not look like you belong. To look young and black is to not belong. Affluence, they believe, is always white. At times when I wander around my neighborhood staring at the dark-skinned nannies, hearing the accents that identify them as immigrants still, I remember this is the world a plantation economy produces—a world where some are bound and others are free, a world of extremes.

Most folks in my predominately white neighborhood see themselves as open-minded; they believe in justice and support the right causes. More often than not, they are social liberals and fiscal conservatives. They may believe in recognizing multiculturalism and celebrating diversity (our neighborhood is full of white gay men and straight white people who have at least one black, Asian, or Hispanic friend), but when it comes to money and class they want to protect what they have, to perpetuate and reproduce it—they want more. The fact that they have so much while others have so little does not cause moral anguish, for they see their good fortune as a sign they are chosen, special, deserving. It enhances their feeling of prosperity and well-being to know everyone cannot live as they do. They scoff at overzealous liberals who are prone to feeling guilty. Downward mobility is a thing of the past; in today's world of affluence, the message is "You got it, flaunt it."

When longtime small family businesses close down because the rents are too high and yet another high-priced gift shop or hair salon opens, they may feel regret but understand this to be the price of economic progress—the price of real estate constantly zooming upward in cost. They have no memories of the days when the West Village was the home of struggling artists, musicians, and poets, a sanctuary for the sexually free and transgressive, a place of rebellion. They have no memory of days when black females could not rent a room or flat here because white folks saw us all, no matter our class, as prostitutes—as bad news. Nowadays we can have the keys to the big house as long as we are coming to clean and do childcare. Neighbors tell me the lack of diversity has nothing to do with racism, it's just a matter of class.

They really believe all black people are poor no matter how many times they laugh at Bill Cosby, salute Colin Powell, mimic Will Smith, dance to Brandy and Whitney Houston, or cheer on Michael Jordan. Yet when the rich black people come to live where they live, they worry that class does not matter enough, for those black folks might have some poor relatives, and there goes the neighborhood. Like the taxi drivers who won't stop because blackness means you are on your way out of the city to Brooklyn—to places that are not safe. They lump all black people together. If rich black people come into the neighborhood, then poor black people will not be far behind.

Black folks with money think about class more than most people do in this society. They know that most of the white people around them believe all black people are poor, even the ones with fancy suits and tailored shirts wearing Rolex watches and carrying leather briefcases. Poverty in the white mind is always primarily black. Even though the white poor are many, living in suburbs and rural areas, they remain invisible. The black poor are everywhere, or so many white people think.

When I am shopping in Barneys, a fancy department store in my neighborhood, and a well-dressed white woman turns to me—even though I am wearing a coat, carrying my handbag, and chatting with a similarly dressed friend—seeking assistance from the first available shopgirl and demands my help, I wonder who and what she sees looking at me. From her perspective she thinks she knows who has class power, who has the right to shop here; the look of the poor and working class is always different from her own. Even if we had been dressed alike she would have looked past attire to see the face of the underprivileged she has been taught to recognize.

In my neighborhood everyone believes the face of poverty is black. The white poor blend in, the black poor stand out. Homeless black males entertain, sing songs, tell jokes, or court attention with kind phrases hoping for money in their cup. Usually white homeless men mumble to themselves or sit silent, a cardboard sign naming their economic pain, separated when they seek help in the mainstream world. At the end of the day black and white indigents often pool earnings, sit side by side, sharing the same bottle, breaking the same bread. At the end of the day they inhabit a world where race and class no longer mean very much.

My other home is in a small midwestern town, a liberal place in the conservative state of Ohio, a state where the Nazi party is growing strong and flags hang in the windows of the patriotic haves and have-nots. It is a racially integrated town, a town with a progressive history, and there is still a neighborly world of caring and sharing. Here, class segregation has been imported from the outside, from a professional-managerial academic class who have come in from northern cities and west coast states and have raised property values. Still, neighborhoods in our small town have greater class and racial diversity than most places in the United States. Racism and sexism exist here, as everywhere. A changing class reality that destabilizes and in some cases will irrevocably alter individual lives is the political shift that threatens. Like everywhere in the Midwest plants are closing; small universities and community colleges are cutting back; full-time employees are "let go" and part-time help is fast becoming a national norm. Class is the pressing issue, but it is not talked about.

The closest most folks can come to talking about class in this nation is to talk about money. For so long everyone has wanted to hold on to the belief that the United States is a class-free society—that anyone who works hard enough can make it to the top. Few people stop to think that in a class-free society there would be no top. While it has always been obvious that some folks have more money than other folks, class difference and classism are rarely overtly apparent, or they are not acknowledged when present. The evils of racism and, much later, sexism, were easier to identify and challenge than the evils of classism. We live in a society where the poor have no public voice. No wonder it has taken so long for many citizens to recognize class—to become class conscious.

Racial solidarity, particularly the solidarity of whiteness, has historically always been used to obscure class, to make the white poor see their interests as one with the world of white privilege. Similarly, the black poor have always been told that class can never matter as much as race. Nowadays the black and white poor know better. They are not so easily duped by an appeal to unquestioned racial identification and solidarity, but they are still uncertain about what all the changes mean; they are uncertain about where they stand.

This uncertainty is shared by those who are not poor, but who could be poor tomorrow if jobs are lost. They, too, are afraid to say how much class matters. While the poor are offered addiction as a way to escape thinking too much, working people are encouraged to shop. Consumer culture silences working people and the middle classes. They are busy buying or planning to buy. Although their fragile hold on economic self-sufficiency is slipping, they still cling to the dream of a class-free society where everyone can make it to the top. They are afraid to face the significance of dwindling resources, the high cost of education, housing, and health care. They are afraid to think too deeply about class.

At the end of the day the threat of class warfare, of class struggle, is just too dangerous to face. The neat binary categories of white and black or male and female are not there when it comes to class. How will they identify the enemy. How will they know who to fear or who to challenge. They cannot see the changing face of global labor—the faces of the women and children whom transnational white supremacist capitalist patriarchy exploits at home and abroad to do dirty work for little pay. They do not speak the languages of the immigrants, male and female, who work here in the meat industry, in clothing sweatshops, as farmworkers, as cooks and busboys, as nannies and domestic workers. Even though the conservative rich daily exploit mass media to teach them that immigrants are the threat, that welfare is the threat, they are starting to wonder about who really profits from poverty, about where the money goes. And whether they like it or not, one day they will have to face the reality: this is not a class-free society.

Oftentimes I too am afraid to think and write about class. I began my journey to class consciousness as a college student learning about the politics of the American left, reading Marx, Fanon, Gramsci, Memmi, the little red book, and so on. But when my studies ended, I still felt my language to be inadequate. I still found it difficult to make sense of class in relation to race and gender. Even now the intellectual left in this nation looks down on anyone who does not speak the chosen jargon. The domain of academic and/or intellectual discourse about class is still mostly white, mostly male. While a few women get to have their say, most of the time men do not really listen. Most leftist men will not fully recognize the left politics of revolutionary feminism: to them class remains the only issue. Within revolutionary feminism a class analysis matters, but so does an analysis of race and gender.

Class matters. Race and gender can be used as screens to deflect attention away from the harsh realities class politics exposes. Clearly, just when we should all be paying attention to class, using race and gender to understand and explain its new dimensions, society, even our government, says let's talk about race and racial injustice. It is impossible to talk meaningfully about ending racism without talking about class. Let us not be duped. Let us not be led by spectacles like the O. J. Simpson trial to believe a mass media, which has always betrayed the cause of racial justice, to think that it was all about race, or it was about gender. Let us acknowledge that first and foremost it was about class and the interlocking nature of race, sex, and class. Let's face the reality that if O. J. Simpson had been poor or even lower-middle class there would have been no media attention. Justice was never the central issue. Our nation's tabloid passion to know about the lives of the rich made class the starting point. It began with money and became a media spectacle that made more money—another case of the rich getting richer. The Simpson trial is credited with upping the GNP by two hundred million dollars. Racism and sexism can be exploited in the interests of class power. Yet no one wants to talk about class. It is not sexy or cute. Better to make it seem that justice is class-free—that what happened to O. J. could happen to any working man.

It has been difficult for black folks to talk about class. Acknowledging class difference destabilizes the notion that racism affects us all in equal ways. It disturbs the illusion of racial solidarity among blacks, used by those individuals with class power to ensure that their class interests will be protected even as they transcend race behind the scenes. When William Julius Wilson first published *The Declining Significance of Race,* his title enraged many readers, especially black folks. Without reading the book, they thought he was saying that race did not matter when what he was prophetically arguing, albeit from a conservative and sometimes liberal standpoint, was that our nation is fast becoming a place where class matters as much as race and oftentimes more.

Feminist theorists acknowledged the overwhelming significance of the interlocking systems of race, gender, and class long before men decided to talk more about these issues together. Yet mainstream culture, particularly mass media, was not willing to tune into a radical political discourse that was not privileging one issue over the other. Class is still often kept separate from race. And while race is often linked with gender, we still lack an ongoing collective public discourse that puts the three together in ways that illuminate for everyone how our nation is organized and what our class politics really are. Women of all races and black people of both genders are fast filling up the ranks of the poor and disenfranchised. It is in our interest to face the issue of class, to become more conscious, to know better so that we can know how best to struggle for economic justice.

I began to write about class in an effort to clarify my own personal journey from a working-class background to the world of affluence, in an effort to be more class conscious. It has been useful to begin with class and work from there. In much of my other work, I have chosen gender or race as a starting point. I choose class now because I believe class warfare will be our nation's fate if we do not collectively challenge classism, if we do not attend to the widening gap between rich and poor, the haves and have-nots. This class conflict is already racialized and gendered. It is already creating division and separation. If the citizens of this nation want to live in a society that is class-free, then we must first work to create an economic system that is just. To work for change, we need to know where we stand.

1

Making the Personal Political: Class in the Family

Living with many bodies in a small space, one is raised with notions of property and privacy quite different from those of people who have always had room. In our house, rooms were shared. Our first house, a rental home, had three bedrooms. It was a concrete block house that had been built as a dwelling for working men who came briefly to this secluded site to search the ground for oil. There were few windows. Dark and cool like a cave, it was a house without memory or history. We did not leave our imprint there. The concrete was too solid to be moved by the details of a couple with three small children and more on the way, trying to create their first home. Situated at the top of a small hill, this house was surrounded by thickets of greenery with wild honeysuckle and blackberry bushes growing everywhere. Behind these thickets rows and rows of crops spread out like blankets. Their stillness and beauty stood out in contrast to the leveled nature surrounding the concrete house—mowed-down grass full of bits and pieces of cement.

Loneliness and fear surrounded this house. A fortress instead of a shelter, it was the perfect place for a new husband, a new father, to build his own patriarchal empire in the home—solid, complete, cold. Architecturally, this house stands out in my memory because of the coolness of the concrete floors. So cold they often made one pull naked feet back under cover, recoiling, like when flesh touches something hot and swiftly pulls away. In a liminal space between the living room and kitchen where a dining room might have been, bunk beds for children were placed. And the children had to learn how to be careful. Falling out of bed could crack one's head wide open, could knock one out cold, leaving flesh as cold as concrete floors. I fell once. That's my imprint: the memory that will not let me forget this house even though we did not live there long.

It lacked too much. There was no bathtub. Water had to be heated, carried, and poured into huge tin tubs. Bathing took place in the kitchen to make this ritual of boiling and pouring and washing take less time. There was no such thing as privacy. Water was scarce, precious, to be used sparingly, and never wasted. Or so the grown-ups told us. This was a better story than the hidden fact that water costs, that too many children running water meant more money to pay. As small children we never thought of cost, of water as a resource. Primitive ecology made us think of it always as magical. It was always precious—to be appreciated and treated with care. We longed to be naked in summer, splashing in plastic pools or playing with hoses, but we knew better. We knew that to leave faucets running was to waste. Water was not to be wasted.

It was a house of concrete blocks put together with stone and cement, a cool house in summer, a cold house in winter—already a harsh landscape. We tried to give this house memories, but it refused to contain them. Impenetrable, the concrete would not hold our stories. Ultimately, we left this house, more bleak and forlorn than before we lived there—a house that would soon be torn down to make way for new housing projects.

There was always a lack of money in our house. As small children we did not know this. Mama was a young fifties mom, her notions of motherhood shaped by magazines and television commercials. Children, she had learned, should not be privy to grown-up concerns, especially grown-up worries. Husband and wife did not discuss or argue in front of children. They waited until children were asleep and talked in their marital bed, voices low, hushed, full of hidden secrets.

I do not know if our mother ever thought of herself as poor or working class. She had come to marriage with our father as a teenage divorcée with two girl children. In those years they lived with their biological father. On weekends they visited with us. Daddy had probably married her because she was pregnant. He was a longtime bachelor, an only child, a mama's boy who could have stayed home forever and used it as the secure site from which to roam and play and be a boy forever. Instead he was trapped by the lures and longings of a beautiful eager young woman more than ten years his junior. He had wanted her even if he had not been sure he wanted to be tied down—unable to roam.

Mama, like her gorgeous sisters and the handsome man she married, loved fun and freedom. She liked to roam. But she also liked playing house. And the concrete box was for her the fulfillment of deep-seated longings. She had finally truly left her mother's house. There would be no going back—no return, no tears, no regret. She was in her second marriage to stay. It was to be the site of her redemption—the second chance on love that would let her dreams be born again. Only mama loved the start of a new life in the concrete box, away from the eyes of a questioning world. Even if the solitude of so much surrounding wilderness threatened, she was secure in the knowledge that she would protect her home—her world—by any means necessary. She was stranded there, on top of a hill, at home with the children. Our daddy, a working man, left early and came home late. His roaming had not ceased. It had merely adjusted itself to the fact of wife and children. Mama, who did not drive, who had no neighbors to chat with, no money to spend, was the wild roaming one who would soon be domesticated—her spirit tamed and broken.

Being poor and working class was never a topic in the concrete box. We were too young to understand class, to share our mother's dreams of moving up and away from the house and family of her origins. A girl without proper education, without the right background, could only change her status through marriage. As a wife she was entitled to respect. All her dreams were about changing her material status, about entering a world where she would have all the trappings of having made it—of having escaped "over home" the tyranny of her mother's house and her mother's ways. In the world's eyes, the folks in that house with their old ways who lived without social security cards, who preferred radio to television, were poor.

Even as small children we knew our father was not pleased with his mother-in-law. He felt she dominated her husband and had taught her daughters that it was fine to do the same thing with the men in their lives. Before marrying he let mama know who would be wearing the pants in his house. It would always be his house.

The house mama was coming from was a rambling two-story wood frame shack with rooms added on according to the temperament of Baba, mama's mother. Already old when we were born, she lived in the house with her husband, our beloved grandfather Daddy Gus. He was everything she was not. A God-fearing, quiet man who followed orders, who never raised his voice or his hand, he was our family saint. Baba was the beloved devil, the fallen angel. Her word was law—a sharp tongue, a quick temper, and the ruthless wit and will needed to make everything go her way.

Unlike the concrete box, the house mama grew up in at 1200 Broad Street was the embodiment of the enchantment of memory. Change was neither needed nor wanted. The old ways of living and being in the world that had lasted were the only ways worth holding onto and sacrificing for. At Baba's house everything that could be made from scratch and not bought in a store was of greater value. It was a house where self-sufficiency was the order of the day. The earth was there for the growing of vegetables and flowers and for the breeding of fishing worms. Little illegal sheds in the back housed chickens for laying fresh eggs. Homegrown grapes grew for making wine, and fruit trees for jam. Butter was churned in this house. Soap was made, odd-shaped chunks made with lye. And cigarettes were rolled with tobacco that had been grown, picked, cured, and made ready for smoking and for twisting and braiding into wreaths by the family, to serve as protection against moths.

This was a house where nothing was ever thrown away and everything had a use. Crowded with objects and memories, there was no way for a child to know that it was the home of grown-ups without social security numbers and regular jobs. Everybody there was always busy. Idleness and self-sufficiency did not go together. All the rooms in this house were crowded with memories; every object had a story to be told by mouths that had lived in the world a long time, mouths that remembered.

Baba's wrath could be incurred by small things, a child touching objects without permission, wanting anything before it was offered by a grown-up. In this house everything was ritual, even the manner of greeting. There was no modern casualness. All rites of remembrance had to be conducted with awareness and respect. One's elders spoke first. A child listened but said nothing. A child waited to be given permission to speak. And whenever a child was out of their place, punishment was required to teach the lesson.

Going to visit or stay at this house was an adventure. There was much to see and do but there was also much that could go wrong. This was the house where everyone lived against the grain. They created their own rules, their own forms of rough justice. It was an unconventional house. That was as true of the architectural plan as it was of the daily habits of its inhabitants. When I was a girl, four people lived in this house of many rooms—Baba and Daddy Gus, Aunt

Margaret (mama's unmarried and childless sister), and Bo (the boy child of a daughter who had died). Everybody had a room of their own—a room reflecting the distinctiveness of their character and their being.

Bo's space was a new addition at the back of the house, small and private. Baba's room was a huge space at the center of the house. It contained her intimate treasures. There was no exploring in this room; it was off limits to anyone save its owner. Then there was the tiny room of Daddy Gus with a small single bed. This was a room full of found treasures—a room with a mattress where one could lie there and look out the window, which went from ceiling to floor. This room was open to the public, and children were the eager public waiting to see what new objects our granddaddy had added to his store of lost and found objects. Upstairs Aunt Margaret lived in a room with sloping ceilings. Her bed was soft, a mound of feather mattresses stacked on top of one another. From girlhood to woman-hood all her treasures lay recklessly tossed about. The bed was rarely made. She liked mess—having everything where it could be seen, a half-filled glass, a half-read letter, a book that had been turned to the same page for more than ten years.

Over home at Baba's house I learned old things were always bet-ter than anything new. Found objects were everywhere. Some were useful, others purely decorative. Every object had a story. Nothing enchanted me more than to hear the history of each everyday object—how it arrived at this particular place. A quiltmaker, Baba was at her best sharing the story of cloth, a quilt made from the cotton dresses of my mother and her sisters, a quilt made from Daddy Gus's suits. A dress first seen in an old photo then the real thing pulled mag-ically out of a trunk somewhere. The object was looked and talked about in two ways—from two perspectives.

Baba did not read or write. Telling a story, listening to a story being told is where knowledge was for her. Conversation is not a place of meaningless chitchat. It is the place where everything must be learned—the site of all epistemology. Over home, everyone is always talking, explaining, illustrating and telling stories with care and excitement. Over home, children can listen to grown-up stories as long as they do not speak. We learn early that there is no place for us in grown-up conversations.

More than any grown-up, Baba taught me about aesthetics, how to really look at things, how to find the inherent beauty. This was a rule in that house; everything, every object, has an element of beauty. Looking deep one sees the beauty and hears the story. Daddy Gus told me that all objects speak. When we really look we can hear the object speak. They believe home is a place where one is enclosed in endless stories. Like arms, they hold and embrace memory. We are only alive in memory. To remember together is the highest form of communion.

Communion with life begins with the earth, and these people, my kin, are people of the earth. They grow things to live. In the front yard herbs and flowers. Delphiniums, tulips, marigolds—all these words I cannot keep inside my head. A swirl of color seized my senses as I walked the stretch of the garden with Baba, as she pushed me in the swing—a swing made with huge braided rope and a board hanging from the tallest tree. There was a story there, about the climbing of the tree, the hanging of the rope, of the possibility of falling.

In the backyard vegetables grew. Scarecrows hung to chase away birds who could clear a field of every crop. My task was to learn how to walk the rows without stepping on growing things. Life was everywhere, under my feet and over my head. The lure of life was everywhere in everything. The first time I dug a fishing worm and watched it move in my hand, feeling the sensual grittiness of mingled dirt and wet, I knew that there is life below and above—always life—that it lures and intoxicates. The chickens laying eggs were such a mystery. We laughed at the way they sat. We laughed at the sounds they made. And we relished being chosen to gather eggs. One must have tender hands to hold eggs, tender words to soothe chickens as they roost.

Everyone in our world talked about race and nobody talked about class. Even though we knew that mama spent her teenage years wanting to run away from this backwoods house and old ways, to have new things, store-bought things, no one talked about class. No one talked about the fact that no one had "real" jobs at 1200 Broad Street, that no one made real money. No one called their lifestyle "alternative" or utopian. Even though it was the 1960s, no one called them hippies. It was just this world where the old ways remained supreme. It was the world of the premodern, the world of poor agrarian southern black landowners living under a regime of racial apartheid. In Baba's world she made the rules, uncaring about what the outside world thought about race or class, or being poor. The first rule of the backwoods is that everybody must think for themselves and listen to what's inside them and follow. That's the reason we have God, Baba used to say. God is above the law.

Living in a world above the absolutes of law and man-made convention was what any black person in their right mind needed to do if they wanted to keep a hold on life. Letting white folks or anybody else control your mind and your body, too, was a surefire way to fail in this life. That's what Baba used to say—may as well kill yourself and be done with it. As a girl I wanted more than anything to live in this world of the old ways. Instead I had to live with mama and the world of the new. Inside me I felt brokenhearted and torn apart. I was an old soul, and the world of the new could never claim me.

I was far away from home before I realized that my smart, work-hard-as-a-janitor-at-the-post-office daddy (who had been in the "colored infantry," fought in wars, and traveled the world) had nothing but stone-cold, hard contempt for these non-reading black folks who lived above the law. A patriotic patriarch, he lived within the law and was proud of it. To mama he openly expressed his contempt of the world she had come from, intensifying her class shame and her longing to move as far away from the old ways as she could without severing all ties. She was always on guard to break the connection if any of her children were getting the idea that they could live on the edge as her parents did, flouting every convention. Lacking the inner strength to live within the old ways, mama needed convention to feel secure. And it was clear to everybody except the inhabitants of the house on Broad Street that the old ways would soon be forgotten. To survive she had to make her peace with the world of the modern and the new. Turning her back on the old ways, she opened her heart and soul to the cheaply made world of the store-bought.

Determined to move on up, mama moved us from the country into the city, out of the concrete box into Mr. Porter's house. Now *that* was a house with history and memory. He had lived to be an old, old man in this house and had died there, his house kept just the way it was when he first moved in, with only the bathroom added on. To mama this house was paradise. A formal dining room, a guest room, a service porch, a big kitchen, a master bedroom downstairs, and two big rooms for the children upstairs. Uninsulated, attic-like rooms had short, sloped ceilings and windows that went from wall to floor. They were cold in winter, impossible to heat. None of that mattered to mama. She was moving into a freshly painted big white house with a lovely front porch.

Built in the early 1900s, Mr. Porter's house was full of possibilities—a house one could dream in. It was never clear what our father thought about this house or the move. No matter where we lived, it would always be his house. His wife and children would always live there because he allowed them to do so. This much was clear. He worked on the house because it was a man's job to do home improvement. We watched in awe as he walled in the side porch, expanding and making a little room that would be my brother's room as well as a storage place.

Like all old houses of this period, there were few closets. There were crawl spaces where stuff could be stored. Closets were not needed in a world where folks possessed the clothes on their backs and a few more items. Now that everyone bought more, bureaus and armoires were needed so that clothing could be stored properly. We had chests of drawers for everyone.

We lived with Mr. Porter's ghosts and his memories in this two-story house with its one added-on bedroom. By then we were a family of six girls, one boy, mama and papa. Away from the lonely house on the hill we had to learn to live with neighbors with watching eyes and whispering tongues. Mama was determined that there should be nothing said against her or her children. We had moved on up into a neighborhood of retired teachers and elderly women and men. We had to learn to behave accordingly.

Still no one talked about class. Mama expressed her appreciation for nice things, her pleasure in her new home, but she did not voice her delight at leaving the old ways behind. Backwoods folks who lived recklessly above the law were not respectable citizens. Seen as crazy and strange, theirs was an outlaw culture—a culture without the tidy rules of middle-class mannerisms, a culture on the edge. Mama refused to live her life on the edge.

In Mr. Porter's house we all became more aware of money. Problems with money, having enough to do what was needed and what was desired, were still never talked about in relation to class. More than anything, like most of the black folks in our neighborhood, we saw money problems as having to do with race, with the fact that white folks kept the good jobs—the well-paying jobs—for themselves. Even though our dad made a decent salary at his job, racial apartheid meant that he could never make the salary a white man made doing the same job. As a black man in the apartheid south he was lucky to have a job with a regular paycheck.

Being the man and making the money gave daddy the right to rule, to decide everything, to overthrow mama's authority at any moment. More than anything else that he hated about married life our dad hated having to share his money. He doled small amounts of money out for household expenses and wanted everything to be accounted for. Determined that there should be no excess for luxury or waste, he made sure that he gave just barely enough to cover expenses. When it came to the material needs of growing children, he took almost everything to be a luxury—from schoolbooks to school clothes. Constantly, we heard the mantra that he had not needed any of these extras (money for band, for gym clothes) growing up. Mostly, he behaved as though these were not his problems.

Mama heard all our material longings. She listened to the pain of our lack. And it was she who tried to give us the desires of our hearts, all the time never talking about class or about her desires to see her children excel in ways that were not open to her. More than class, mama saw sexuality—the threat of unwanted pregnancy—as the path that closed all options for a female. While she never encouraged her daughters to think about marrying men with money, she used the threat of ruin as a way to warn us away from sexuality. And she constantly urged us to keep our minds on getting an education so we could get good jobs.

Her task was not easy. Daddy believed a woman with too much education would never find a husband. In the dark when they talked lying in bed, away from the ears of children, he warned and berated her. She had to train her daughters to be the kind of girls men would want to marry—quiet, obedient, good homemakers—and at the same time secretly share with us that we needed to prepare ourselves to work. Sex and race were the dangers that made it possible for a girl to get off track, to get lost, and never be found again; no one talked about class.

Women who received assistance from the state—women on welfare—were to be pitied not because they did not have jobs but because they did not have men to provide for them, men who would make them respectable. During my sweet sixteen years I began to feel in my flesh that being respectable and getting respect were not one and the same. Anyone listening to Aretha knew that. Respect was about being seen and treated like you matter. Men like my daddy did not respect women. To them a woman could be bought like any other object; what was there to respect?

The only respectable women who lived alone in our communities were schoolteachers. Nobody expected them to marry. After all they were the women who had chosen mind over matter. They had chosen to become women no man would desire—women who think. While they lived in nice houses and seemed not to suffer material want, they were still pitied. Unlike women on welfare they had to remain childless to maintain respect. They had to live alone in a world that believed nothing was more tragic than a woman alone.

Mama taught me to admire these women and seek to be like them, to cultivate my mind. And it was mama who let me know that cultivating the mind could place one outside the boundaries of desire. Inside the space of heterosexual desire a woman had to be dependent on a man for everything. All the working black women in our lives wanted to be able to stay home and spend money—the money men would make for them working in the tobacco fields, in the mines, doing hard labor. Men on our street who worked in the coal mines came home covered in a thin layer of grayish white dust that looked like ash. Women looked at them and talked about how they made the only really good money a working black man could make. No one talked of the dangers; it was the money that mattered.

Even as we sat next to the children of black doctors, lawyers, and undertakers in our segregated schoolrooms, no one talked about class. When those children were treated better, we thought it was because they were prettier, smarter, and just knew the right way to act. Our mother was obsessed with teaching us how to do things right, teaching us manners and bourgeois decorum. Yet she had not been around enough middle-class black people to know what to do. She fashioned a middle-class sensibility by watching television, reading magazines, or looking at the ways of the white folks she cleaned houses for now and then. It was only now and then, and only after her children were in their teens, that she was allowed by daddy to work outside the home. She slaved outside the home for extras, for icing on the cake, to give her children the little special things we longed for. Her work was sacrificial. It never counted as real work. Then there were the middle-class black people she encountered at church. Imitating them was one way to become like them. She watched, observed, admired, then imposed these visions on her children, all the while never mentioning the word *class.*

Money was necessary and important. Everybody talked about money, nobody talked about class. Like most southern cities where racial apartheid remained the order of the day long after laws were on the books championing desegregation, black people lived on one side of the tracks and white folks on the other. Legalized desegregation did not change that. No matter how much money anybody black could make, they were still confined to the black spaces. This arrangement made it seem that we were truly living in a world where class did not matter; race mattered. Money mattered. But no amount of money could change the color of one's skin. Everyone held on to the belief that race was the factor that meant all black people shared the same fate no matter how much their worth in dollars.

While class was never talked about in our household, the importance of work—of working hard—was praised. Our father worked hard at his job and mama worked hard in the home. Hard work was a virtue. As children we heard again and again that idleness was dangerous. At church we were told to "work while it is day for the night cometh when no man can work." My father and his buddies talked about hierarchies in the world of work, expressing their rage at bosses who did little but were better paid. Overhearing these conversations in my teens I felt uneasy being a witness to male pain. Even then, race was still the factor highlighted most. The bosses were white. Unions were there to protect white jobs and white workers. Nobody cared about black men.

Black men who could not find work could join the military. Living near a military base meant that we were always aware of the military as a place of employment. Black boys who were wayward went into the military. Everyone was confident that the discipline and hard work the military demanded would straighten out any man-child walking a crooked path and give him a good paycheck, one that would let him send money home. A military man who had served his time, our father believed that the military made a male disciplined and tough. The useful lessons learned there could last a lifetime despite the racism. Since one could spend a lifetime working in the military, it was the one place where black males could count on keeping a job. Black men left the military and found that it was hard to find work. It took awhile for our daddy to find a good job as a janitor at the post office. And when he did it was a source of pride to be a hard worker, to be employed at the same place for one's entire working life. This is the legacy I inherited from him, a belief in the integrity of hard work—a respect for the worker.

Through his experience we learned to be proud of being working class even though our conversations about class were always tied to race. To know ourselves fully we had to find our place in the world of work, and that, ultimately, meant confronting race and class.

2

Coming to Class Consciousness

As a child I often wanted things money could buy that my parents could not afford and would not get. Rather than tell us we did not get some material thing because money was lacking, mama would frequently manipulate us in an effort to make the desire go away. Sometimes she would belittle and shame us about the object of our desire. That's what I remember most. That lovely yellow dress I wanted would become in her storytelling mouth a really ugly mammy-made thing that no girl who cared about her looks would desire. My desires were often made to seem worthless and stupid. I learned to mistrust and silence them. I learned that the more clearly I named my desires, the more unlikely those desires would ever be fulfilled.

I learned that my inner life was more peaceful if I did not think about money, or allow myself to indulge in any fantasy of desire. I learned the art of sublimation and repression. I learned it was better to make do with acceptable material desires than to articulate the unacceptable. Before I knew money mattered, I had often chosen objects to desire that were costly, things a girl of my class would not ordinarily desire. But then I was still a girl who was unaware of class, who did not think my desires were stupid and wrong. And when I found they were I let them go. I concentrated on survival, on making do.

When I was choosing a college to attend, the issue of money surfaced and had to be talked about. While I would seek loans and scholarships, even if everything related to school was paid for, there would still be transportation to pay for, books, and a host of other hidden costs. Letting me know that there was no extra money to be had, mama urged me to attend any college nearby that would offer financial aid. My first year of college I went to a school close to home. A plain-looking white woman recruiter had sat in our living room and explained to my parents that everything would be taken care of, that I would be awarded a full academic scholarship, that they would have to pay nothing. They knew better. They knew there was still transportation, clothes, all the hidden costs. Still they found this school acceptable. They could drive me there and pick me up. I would not need to come home for holidays. I could make do.

After my parents dropped me at the predominately white women's college, I saw the terror in my roommate's face that she was going to be housed with someone black, and I requested a change. She had no doubt also voiced her concern. I was given a tiny single room by the stairs—a room usually denied a first-year student—but I was a first-year black student, a scholarship girl who could never in a million years have afforded to pay her way or absorb the cost of a single room. My fellow students kept their distance from me. I ate in the cafeteria and did not have to worry about who would pay for pizza and drinks in the world outside. I kept my desires to myself, my lacks and my loneliness; I made do.

I rarely shopped. Boxes came from home, with brand-new clothes mama had purchased. Even though it was never spoken she did not want me to feel ashamed among privileged white girls. I was the only black girl in my dorm. There was no room in me for shame. I felt contempt and disinterest. With their giggles and their obsession to marry,

the white girls at the women's college were aliens. We did not reside on
the same planet. I lived in the world of books. The one white woman
who became my close friend found me there reading. I was hiding
under the shadows of a tree with huge branches, the kinds of trees that
just seemed to grow effortlessly on well-to-do college campuses. I sat
on the "perfect" grass reading poetry, wondering how the grass around
me could be so lovely and yet when daddy had tried to grow grass in
the front yard of Mr. Porter's house it always turned yellow or brown
and then died. Endlessly, the yard defeated him, until finally he gave up.
The outside of the house looked good but the yard always hinted at
the possibility of endless neglect. The yard looked poor.

Foliage and trees on the college grounds flourished. Greens were
lush and deep. From my place in the shadows I saw a fellow student
sitting alone weeping. Her sadness had to do with all the trivia that
haunted our day's classwork, the fear of not being smart enough, of
losing financial aid (like me she had loans and scholarships, though
her family paid some), and boys. Coming from an Illinois family of
Czechoslovakian immigrants she understood class.

When she talked about the other girls who flaunted their wealth
and family background there was a hard edge of contempt, anger, and
envy in her voice. Envy was always something I pushed away from
my psyche. Kept too close for comfort envy could lead to infatuation
and on to desire. I desired nothing that they had. She desired everything, speaking her desires openly without shame. Growing up in the
kind of community where there was constant competition to see
who could buy the bigger better whatever, in a world of organized
labor, of unions and strikes, she understood a world of bosses and
workers, of haves and have-nots.

White friends I had known in high school wore their class privilege modestly. Raised, like myself, in church traditions that taught us
to identify only with the poor, we knew that there was evil in excess.
We knew rich people were rarely allowed into heaven. God had
given them a paradise of bounty on earth and they had not shared.

The rare ones, the rich people who shared, were the only ones able to meet the divine in paradise, and even then it was harder for them to find their way. According to the high school friends we knew, flaunting wealth was frowned upon in our world, frowned upon by God and community.

The few women I befriended my first year in college were not wealthy. They were the ones who shared with me stories of the other girls flaunting the fact that they could buy anything expensive— clothes, food, vacations. There were not many of us from working class backgrounds; we knew who we were. Most girls from poor backgrounds tried to blend in, or fought back by triumphing over wealth with beauty or style or some combination of the above. Being black made me an automatic outsider. Holding their world in contempt pushed me further to the edge. One of the fun things the "in" girls did was choose someone and trash their room. Like so much else deemed cute by insiders, I dreaded the thought of strangers entering my space and going through my things. Being outside the in crowd made me an unlikely target. Being contemptuous made me first on the list. I did not understand. And when my room was trashed it unleashed my rage and deep grief over not being able to protect my space from violation and invasion. I hated that girls who had so much, took so much for granted, never considered that those of us who did not have mad money would not be able to replace broken things, perfume poured out, or talcum powder spread everywhere— that we did not know everything could be taken care of at the dry cleaner's because we never took our clothes there. My rage fueled by contempt was deep, strong, and long lasting. Daily it stood as a challenge to their fun, to their habits of being.

Nothing they did to win me over worked. It came as a great surprise. They had always believed black girls wanted to be white girls, wanted to possess their world. My stoney gaze, silence, and absolute refusal to cross the threshold of their world was total mystery; it was for them a violation they needed to avenge. After trashing my room, they tried to win me over with apologies and urges to talk and understand. There was nothing about me I wanted them to understand. Everything about their world was overexposed, on the surface.

One of my English professors had attended Stanford University. She felt that was the place for me to go—a place where intellect was valued over foolish fun and games and dress up, and finding a husband did not overshadow academic work. She had gone to Stanford. I had never thought about the state of California. Getting my parents to agree to my leaving Kentucky to attend a college in a nearby state had been hard enough. They had accepted a college they could reach by car, but a college thousands of miles away was beyond their imagination. Even I had difficulty grasping going that far away from home. The lure for me was the promise of journeying and arriving at a destination where I would be accepted and understood.

All the barely articulated understandings of class privilege that I had learned my first year of college had not hipped me to the reality of class shame. It still had not dawned on me that my parents, especially mama, resolutely refused to acknowledge any difficulties with money because her sense of shame around class was deep and intense. And when this shame was coupled with her need to feel that she had risen above the low-class backwoods culture of her family, it was impossible for her to talk in a straightforward manner about the strains it would put on the family for me to attend Stanford.

All I knew then was that, as with all my desires, I was told that this desire was impossible to fulfill. At first it was not talked about in relation to money, it was talked about in relation to sin. California was an evil place, a modern-day Babylon where souls were easily seduced away from the path of righteousness. It was not a place for an innocent young girl to go on her own. Mama brought the message back that my father had absolutely refused to give permission.

I expressed my disappointment through ongoing unrelenting grief. I explained to mama that other parents wanted their children to go to good schools. It still had not dawned on me that my parents knew nothing about "good" schools. Even though I knew mama had not graduated from high school I still held her in awe. Mama and daddy were awesome authority figures—family fascists of a very high order. As children we knew that it was better not to doubt their word or their knowledge. We blindly trusted them.

A crucial aspect of our family fascism was that we were not allowed much contact with other families. We were rarely allowed to go to someone's house. We knew better than to speak about our family in other people's homes. While we caught glimpses of different habits of being, different ways of doing things in other families, we knew that to speak of those ways at our home, to try to use them to influence or change our parents, was to risk further confinement.

Our dad had traveled to foreign countries as a soldier but he did not speak of these experiences. Safety, we had been religiously taught in our household, was always to be found close to home. We were not a family who went on vacations, who went exploring. When relatives from large cities would encourage mama to let us children go back with them, their overtures were almost always politely refused. Once mama agreed that I could go to Chicago to visit an elderly cousin, Schuyler—a name strange and beautiful on our lips.

Retired Cousin Schuyler lived a solitary life in a basement flat of the brownstone he shared with Lovie, his wife of many years. Vocationally a painter, he did still lifes and nudes. When they came to visit us, Mama had shown them the painting I had done that won a school prize. It was a portrait of a poor lonely boy with sad eyes. Despite our class background all of us took art classes in school. By high school the disinterested had forgotten about art and only those of us who were committed to doing art, to staying close to an artistic environment, remained. For some that closeness was just a kindly voyeurism. They had talent but were simply not sufficiently interested to use it. Then there were folks like me, full of passion and talent, but without the material resources to do art. Making art was for people with money.

I understood this when my parents adamantly refused to have my painting framed. Only framed work could be in the show. My art teacher, an Italian immigrant who always wore black, showed me how to make a frame from pieces of wood found in the trash. Like my granddaddy he was a lover of found objects. Both of them were men without resources who managed to love beauty and survive. In high school art classes we talked about beauty—about aesthetics. But it was after class that I told the teacher how I had learned these things already from my grandmother.

Each year students would choose an artist and study their work and then do work in that same tradition. I chose abstract expressionism and the work of Willem de Kooning. Choosing to paint a house in autumn, the kind of house I imagined living in, with swirls of color—red, yellow, brown—I worked for hours after class, trying to give this house the loneliness I felt inside. This painting was my favorite. I showed it to Cousin Schuyler along with the image of the lonely boy.

It remains a mystery how Schuyler and Lovie convinced mama that it would be fine to let me spend some time with them in Chicago—my first big city. Traveling to Chicago was my first sojourn out of the apartheid south. It was my first time in a world where I saw black people working at all types of jobs. They worked at the post office delivering mail, in factories, driving buses, collecting garbage—black people with good jobs. This new world was awesome. It was a world where black people had power. I worked in a little store owned by a black male friend of my aunt. The wife of this friend had her own beauty parlor but no children. They had money.

Lovie talked to me about class. There were low-class folks one should not bother with. She insisted one should aim high. These were big city ideas. In our small town community we had been taught to see everyone as worthy. Mama especially preached that you should never see yourself as better than anyone, that no matter anyone's lot in life they deserved respect. Mama preached this even though she aimed high. These messages confused me. The big city was too awesome and left me afraid.

Yet it also changed my perspective, for it had shown me a world where black people could be artists. And what I saw was that artists barely survived. No one in my family wanted me to pursue art; they wanted me to get a good job, to be a teacher. Painting was something to do when real work was done. Once, maybe twice even, I expressed my desire to be an artist. That became an occasion for dire warning and laughter, since like so many desires it was foolish, hence the laughter. Since foolish girls are likely to do foolish things dire warnings had to come after the laughter. Black folks could not make a living as artists. They pointed to the one example—the only grown-up black artist they knew, Cousin Schuyler, living in a dark basement like some kind of mole or rat.

Like everything else the choice to be an artist was talked about in terms of race, not class. The substance of the warnings was always to do with the untalked-about reality of class in America. I did not think about being an artist anymore. I struggled with the more immediate question of where to continue college, of how to find a place where I would not feel like such an alien.

When my parents refused to permit me to attend Stanford, I accepted the verdict for awhile. Overwhelmed by grief, I could barely speak for weeks. Mama intervened and tried to change my father's mind as folks she respected in the outside world told her what a privilege it was for me to have this opportunity, that Stanford University was a good school for a smart girl. Without their permission I decided I would go. And even though she did not give her approval mama was willing to help.

My decision made conversations about money necessary. Mama explained that California was too far away, that it would always "cost" to get there, that if something went wrong they would not be able to come and rescue me, that I would not be able to come home for holidays. I heard all this but its meaning did not sink in. I was just relieved I would not be returning to the women's college, to the place where I had truly been an outsider.

There were other black students at Stanford. There was even a dormitory where many black students lived. I did not know I could choose to live there. I went where I was assigned. Going to Stanford was the first time I flew somewhere. Only mama stood and waved farewell as I left to take the bus to the airport. I left with a heavy heart, feeling both excitement and dread. I knew nothing about the world I was journeying to. Not knowing made me afraid but my fear of staying in place was greater.

Since we do not talk about class in this society and since information is never shared or talked about freely in a fascist family, I had no idea what was ahead of me. In small ways I was ignorant. I had never been on an escalator, a city bus, an airplane, or a subway. I arrived in San Francisco with no understanding that Palo Alto was a long drive away—that it would take money to find transportation there. I decided to take the city bus. With all my cheap overpacked bags I must have seemed like just another innocent immigrant when I struggled to board the bus.

This was a city bus with no racks for luggage. It was filled with immigrants. English was not spoken. I felt lost and afraid. Without words the strangers surrounding me understood the universal language of need and distress. They reached for my bags, holding and helping. In return I told them my story—that I had left my village in the South to come to Stanford University, that like them my family were workers, they worked the land—they worked in the world. They were workers. They understood workers. I would go to college and learn how to make a world where they would not have to work so hard.

When I arrived at my destination, the grown-ups in charge cautioned me about trusting strangers, telling me what I already knew, that I was no longer in my town, that nothing was the same. On arriving I called home. Before I could speak, I began to weep as I heard the far-away sound of mama's voice. I tried to find the words, to slow down, to tell her how it felt to be a stranger, to speak my uncertainty and longing. She told me this is the lot I had chosen. I must live with it. After her words there was only silence. She had hung up on me—let me go into this world where I am a stranger still.

Stanford University was a place where one could learn about class from the ground up. Built by a man who believed in hard work, it was to have been a place where students of all classes would come, women and men, to work together and learn. It was to be a place of equality and communalism. His vision was seen by many as almost communist. The fact that he was rich made it all less threatening. Perhaps no one really believed the vision could be realized. The university was named after his son who had died young, a son who had carried his name but who had no future money could buy. No amount of money can keep death away. But it could keep memory alive. And so we work and learn in buildings that remind us of a young son carried away by death too soon, of a father's unrelenting grief remembered.

Everything in the landscape of my new world fascinated me, the plants brought from a rich man's travels all over the world back to this place of water and clay. At Stanford University adobe buildings blend with Japanese plum trees and leaves of kumquat. On my way to study medieval literature, I ate my first kumquat. Surrounded by flowering cactus and a South American shrub bougainvillea of such trailing beauty it took my breath away, I was in a landscape of dreams, full of hope and possibility. If nothing else would hold me, I would not remain a stranger to the earth. The ground I stood on would know me.

Class was talked about behind the scenes. The sons and daughters from rich, famous, or notorious families were identified. The grown-ups in charge of us were always looking out for a family who might give their millions to the college. At Stanford my classmates wanted to know me, thought it hip, cute, and downright exciting to have a black friend. They invited me on the expensive vacations and ski trips I could not afford. They offered to pay. I never went. Along with other students who were not from privileged families, I searched for places to go during the holiday times when the dormitory was closed. We got together and talked about the assumption that everyone had money to travel and would necessarily be leaving. The staff would be on holiday as well, so all students had to leave. Now and then the staff did not leave and we were allowed to stick around. Once, I went home with one of the women who cleaned for the college.

Now and then when she wanted to make extra money mama would work as a maid. Her decision to work outside the home was seen as an act of treason by our father. At Stanford I was stunned to find that there were maids who came by regularly to vacuum and tidy our rooms. No one had ever cleaned up behind me and I did not want them to. At first I roomed with another girl from a working-class background—a beautiful white girl from Orange County who looked like pictures I had seen on the cover of *Seventeen* magazine. Her mother had died of cancer during her high school years and she had since been raised by her father. She had been asked by the college officials if she would find it problematic to have a black roommate. A scholarship student like myself, she knew her preferences did not matter and as she kept telling me, she did not really care.

Like my friend during freshman year she shared the understanding of what it was like to be a have-not in a world of haves. But unlike me she was determined to become one of them. If it meant she had to steal nice clothes to look the same as they did, she had no problem taking these risks. If it meant having a privileged boyfriend who left bruises on her body now and then, it was worth the risk. Cheating was worth it. She believed the world the privileged had created was all unfair—all one big cheat; to get ahead one had to play the game. To her I was truly an innocent, a lamb being led to the slaughter. It did not surprise her one bit when I began to crack under the pressure of contradictory values and longings.

Like all students who did not have seniority, I had to see the school psychiatrists to be given permission to live off campus. Unaccustomed to being around strangers, especially strangers who did not share or understand my values, I found the experience of living in the dorms difficult. Indeed, almost everyone around me believed working-class folks had no values. At the university where the founder, Leland Stanford, had imagined different classes meeting on common ground, I learned how deeply individuals with class privilege feared and hated the working classes. Hearing classmates express contempt and hatred toward people who did not come from the right backgrounds shocked me. Naively, I believed them to be so young to hold those views, so devoid of life experiences that would serve to uphold or make sense of these thoughts. I had always worked. Working-class people had always encouraged and supported me.

To survive in this new world of divided classes, this world where I was also encountering for the first time a black bourgeois elite that was as contemptuous of working people as their white counterparts were, I had to take a stand, to get clear my own class affiliations. This was the most difficult truth to face. Having been taught all my life to believe that black people were inextricably bound in solidarity by our struggles to end racism, I did not know how to respond to elitist black people who were full of contempt for anyone who did not share their class, their way of life.

At Stanford I encountered for the first time a black diaspora. Of the few black professors present, the vast majority were from African or Caribbean backgrounds. Elites themselves, they were only interested in teaching other elites. Poor folks like myself, with no background to speak of, were invisible. We were not seen by them or anyone else. Initially, I went to all meetings welcoming black students, but when I found no one to connect with I retreated. In the shadows I had time and books to teach me about the nature of class—about the ways black people were divided from themselves.

Despite this rude awakening, my disappointment at finding myself estranged from the group of students I thought would understand, I still looked for connections. I met an older black male graduate student who also came from a working-class background. Even though he had gone to the right high school, a California school for gifted students, and then to Princeton as an undergraduate, he understood intimately the intersections of race and class. Good in sports and in the classroom, he had been slotted early on to go far, to go where other black males had not gone. He understood the system. Academically, he fit. Had he wanted to, he could have been among the elite but he chose to be on the margins, to hang with an intellectual artistic avant garde. He wanted to live in a world of the mind where there was no race or class. He wanted to worship at the throne of art and knowledge. He became my mentor, comrade, and companion.

When we were not devoting ourselves to books and to poetry we confronted a real world where we were in need of jobs. Even though I taught an occasional class, I worked in the world of the mundane. I worked at a bookstore, cooked at a club, worked for the telephone company. My way out of being a maid, of doing the dirty work of cleaning someone else's house, was to become a schoolteacher. The thought terrified me. From grade school on I feared and hated the classroom. In my imagination it was still the ultimate place of inclusion and exclusion, discipline and punishment—worse than the fascist family because there was no connection of blood to keep in check impulses to search and destroy.

Now and then a committed college professor opened my mind to the reality that the classroom could be a place of passion and possibility, but, in general, at the various colleges I attended it was the place where the social order was kept in place. Throughout my graduate student years, I was told again and again that I lacked the proper decorum of a graduate student, that I did not understand my place. Slowly I began to understand fully that there was no place in academe for folks from working-class backgrounds who did not wish to leave the past behind. That was the price of the ticket. Poor students would be welcome at the best institutions of higher learning only if they were willing to surrender memory, to forget the past and claim the assimilated present as the only worthwhile and meaningful reality.

Students from nonprivileged backgrounds who did not want to forget often had nervous breakdowns. They could not bear the weight of all the contradictions they had to confront. They were crushed. More often than not they dropped out with no trace of their inner anguish recorded, no institutional record of the myriad ways their take on the world was assaulted by an elite vision of class and privilege. The records merely indicated that even after receiving financial aid and other support, these students simply could not make it, simply were not good enough.

At no time in my years as a student did I march in a graduation ceremony. I was not proud to hold degrees from institutions where I had been constantly scorned and shamed. I wanted to forget these experiences, to erase them from my consciousness. Like a prisoner set free I did not want to remember my years on the inside. When I finished my doctorate I felt too much uncertainty about who I had become. Uncertain about whether I had managed to make it through without giving up the best of myself, the best of the values I had been raised to believe in—hard work, honesty, and respect for everyone no matter their class—I finished my education with my allegiance to the working class intact. Even so, I had planted my feet on the path leading in the direction of class privilege. There would always be contradictions to face. There would always be confrontations around the issue of class. I would always have to reexamine where I stand.

3

Class and the Politics of Living Simply

At church we were taught to identify with the poor. This was the spoken narrative of class that dominated my growing-up years. The poor were chosen and closer to the heart of the divine because their lives embodied the wisdom of living simply. By the time I was in junior high school, I was reading to my church congregation during the morning offering, choosing scriptures from the biblical Book of Matthew, which admonished believers to recognize our oneness with the poor and all who are lacking the means for material well-being. I read from the twenty-fifth book of Matthew passages describing a day when we stand before the divine and all the angels seated with him in heavenly glory.

On that day of reckoning, scriptures shared, "all the nations will be gathered before him." In the presence of witnesses, joined in common community, those who had identified with and cared for the poor and needy would be chosen to dwell among the godly. Those who were not chosen were to be told: "Depart from me, you who are cursed, into the eternal fire prepared for the devil and his angels. For I was hungry and you gave me nothing to eat, I was thirsty and you gave me nothing to drink. I was a stranger and you did not invite me in, I needed clothes and you did not clothe me, I was sick and in prison and you did not look after me." Questioning this decision, the unchosen answer: "Lord, when did we see you hungry or thirsty or a stranger or needing clothes or sick or in prison and did not help you?" He replies: "I tell you the truth, whatever you did not do for one of the least of these, you did not do for me." To not identify with the poor and the downtrodden, to fail to attend to their needs, was to suffer the pain of being disinherited.

I was not allowed to stand before my church community and read these scriptures until it was clear that I understood in mind and heart their meaning. Individuals who have declared their faith, who walk on a spiritual path, choose identification with the poor. In that same book of the Bible we were taught to give to those less fortunate discreetly with no thought of personal glory or gain. To not be discreet might call attention to those who suffered lack and they might be ridiculed, scorned, or shamed. The best way to give was to give secretly so there could be no question of return or obligation.

Again and again we were told in church that once we crossed the threshold of this holy place sanctified by divine spirit we were all one. As a child I did not know who the poor were among us. I did not understand that as a family of seven children and two adults living on one working-class income, when it came to the issue of material resources we were at times poor. Sharing resources was commonplace in our world—a direct outcome of a belief in the necessity of claiming the poor as ourselves.

Indeed showing solidarity with the poor was essential spiritual work, a way to learn the true meaning of community and enact the sharing of resources that would necessarily dismantle hierarchy and difference. In the community of my upbringing no one talked about capitalism. We knew the word *communism* because keeping the world safe for democracy was discussed. And communism was the identified threat. No one talked about the way capitalism worked, the fact that it demanded that there be surplus labor creating conditions for widespread unemployment. No one talked about slavery as an institution paving the way for advanced capitalist economic growth.

In his discussion of the impact of capitalism as a force shaping our basic assumptions about life, "Naming Our Gods," David Hilfiker emphasizes the way in which commitment to Christian ethics directly challenges allegiance to any economic system that encourages one group to have and hoard material plenty while others do without. Working as a physician caring for the inner city poor he states: "Our work is grounded in the understanding that God calls us to care for and move into solidarity with those who have been—for whatever reason—excluded from society."

Throughout my childhood I saw embodied in our home and in the community as a whole the belief that resources should be shared. When mama would send us to neighbors with food or clothes we complained, just as we complained when she sent us to collect the gifts that were sometimes given to us by caring folks who recognized the material strains of raising a large family on one income, especially since patriarchal heads of households, like our dad, often kept much of their paycheck for their own private use. Women in our community understood this and had the best networks for figuring out ways to give and share with others without causing embarrassment or shame.

There was necessarily a tension between the call to identify with the poor and the recognition that in the secular world of our everyday life, the poor were often subjected to harassments and humiliations that generated shame. Despite the valorization of the poor in religious life, no one really wanted to be poor. No one wanted to be the object of pity or shame. Writing about the impact of shame on our sense of self in *Coming Out of Shame,* Gershen Kaufman and Lev Raphael share this insight: "Unexamined shame on either the individual or societal level becomes an almost insurmountable obstacle to the realization of inner wholeness and true connection with others, because shame reveals us all as lesser, worthless, deficient—in a word, profoundly and unspeakably inferior." On one hand, from a spiritual perspective, we were taught to think of the poor as the chosen ones, closer to the divine, ever worthy in the sight of God, but on the other hand, we knew that in the real world being poor was never considered a blessing. The fact that being poor was seen as a cause for shame prevented it from being an occasion for celebration.

Solidarity with the poor was the gesture that intervened on shame. It was to be expressed not just by treating the poor well and with generosity but by living as simply as one could. If you were well off, choosing to live simply meant you had more to share with those who were not as fortunate. David Hilfiker describes an earlier time in our history as a nation when it was just assumed that a physician would care for the poor. However, in more recent times Hilfiker finds himself regarded almost as a "saint" because he chooses to work with the poor. Yet he shares this insight: "This perception of my extraordinary sacrifice persists even though I've mentioned in my talk that Marja's and my combined income (around $45,000) puts us well above the median income of this county, and I've made clear that we reap the benefits of community and meaningful vocations in ways most people only dream of." The call to live simply is regarded by most people as foolhardy. Most folks think that to play it safe, one must strive to accumulate as much material wealth as possible and hoard it.

In the late fifties and sixties, our nation had not yet become a place where the poor would be regarded solely with contempt. In the growing-up years of my life, my siblings and I were constantly told that it was a sin to place ourselves above others. We were taught that material possessions told you nothing about the inner life of another human being, whether they were loving, a person of courage and integrity. We were told to look past material trappings and find the person inside. It was easy to do this in childhood, in the small community where we were raised and knew our neighbors.

My college years were the time in my life where I was more directly confronted with the issue of class. Like many students from working-class backgrounds seeking upward mobility, prior to this time I had no personal contact with rich people. All my notions of higher education were informed by a romantic vision of intellectual hard work and camaraderie. I, like most of my working-class peers, was not prepared to face the class hierarchies present in academia, or the way information in the classroom was slanted to protect the interests of ruling class groups. Offering testimony of a similar experience in the collection *Strangers in Paradise: Academics from the Working Class,* Karl Anderson writes about the shock he experienced in graduate school engendered by his "discovery of the greed that dominated the consciousness of the majority of my peers and professors." Like many of us, he remembers that "social class was, of course, almost never mentioned," even in classes with literature focusing on the poor and working class. When class was mentioned at the school I attended, negative stereotypes about poor and working-class people were the only perspectives evoked.

When I went to fancy colleges where money and status defined one's place in the scheme of things, I found myself an object of curiosity, ridicule, and even contempt from my classmates because of my class background. At times I felt class shame. Often, that shame arose around food—when I did not know what certain foods were that everyone else was familiar with. That shame came and went. But in its wake I was left with the realization that my fellow students had no desire to understand anything about the lives of working-class people. They did not want to know or identify with the poor. And they were, above all, not interested in solidarity with the poor.

Students who considered themselves socialists were not so much interested in the poor as they were desirous of leading the poor, of being their guides and saviors. It was just this paternalism toward the poor that the vision of solidarity I had learned in religious settings was meant to challenge. From a spiritual perspective, the poor were there to guide and lead the rest of us by example if not by outright action and testimony. As a student I read Marx, Gramsci, and a host of other male thinkers on the subject of class. These works provided theoretical paradigms but rarely offered tools for confronting the complexity of class in daily life.

The work of liberation theologists moved in a direction I could understand. While leftist thought often provided the theoretical back-drop for this work, it focused more pointedly on the concrete relations between those who have and those who have not. Progressive theology stressed the importance of solidarity with the poor that I had learned growing up—a solidarity that was to be expressed by word and deed. David Hilfiker's piece echoes this theology when he urges us to consider the ways identification with wealth has produced a culture where belief in an oppressive capitalism functions like a religion. He contends: "It is important for us to understand that we have chosen this. Neither modern capitalism nor economic impera-tive requires that necessities be distributed according to wealth. Today's 'capitalistic' economic systems can easily be modified through taxation and wealth-transfer programs, such as Social Security, to provide necessities." Sharing resources is no longer deemed an impor-tant value by most citizens of our nation. In his insightful book *Freedom of Simplicity,* Richard Foster expresses the vision of soli-darity at the heart of Christian teachings about poverty. He writes: "In the twelfth chapter of Romans, Paul sets forth a lovely picture of a community of people living in simplicity. Placed in the context of teaching on the gifts of the Holy Spirit, Paul provides a profoundly practical understanding of how we are to live. We are to give freely to the needs of the saints and to practice ordinary hospitality. We are to enter into the needs of one another—rejoicing with those who rejoice and weeping with those who weep. We are to deal with class and status distinction to the extent that we can be freely among the lowly." This vision of living simply captured the imagination of Americans who wanted to live in an alternative way during the sixties and seventies but began to have less impact as an ethos of hedonistic consumption swept the nation in the eighties.

At one time the vast majority of this nation's citizens were schooled in religious doctrine which emphasized the danger of wealth, greed, and covetousness. Just as many of us were raised to stand in solidarity with the poor, we were raised to believe that the pursuit of wealth was dangerous, not because riches made one bad but because they could lead one down a path of self-interested pathological narcissism. Anyone walking on such a path would necessarily be estranged from community. Religious teaching reminds us that profit cannot be the sole measure of value in life. In the biblical Book of Matthew we were taught: "What good will it be for a man if he gains the whole world, yet loses his soul?"

As a nation, a shift in attitudes toward the poor began to happen in the seventies. Suddenly notions of communalism were replaced with notions of self-interest. The idea that everyone could become rich simply by working hard or finding a gimmick gained public acceptance as contemptuous attitudes toward the poor began to permeate all aspects of our culture. Changing attitudes toward the poor corresponded with the devaluation of traditional religious beliefs. While new age spiritual thought gathered momentum, it too tended to "blame" the poor for their plight and exonerate the rich.

Much new age thought actually reversed traditional Christian condemnation of the hoarding of wealth by stressing not only that the poor had freely chosen to be poor (since we live many lives and choose our status and fate), but that economic prosperity was a sign of divine blessing. A critique of greed does not enter into much new age thinking about wealth. Discourses of greed and exploitation are rarely evoked. In worst-case scenarios in new age writing, the rich are encouraged to believe that they have no responsibility for the fate of the poor and disenfranchised since we have all chosen our lot in life.

Significantly, while the uncaring rich and powerful, especially those in control of government, big business, and mass media, were and are at the forefront of campaigns to place all accountability for poverty on the poor and to equate being poor with being worthless, lots of other nonwealthy citizens have allied themselves with these groups. This denigration of the poor has been most graphically expressed by ongoing attacks on the welfare system and the plans to dismantle it without providing economic alternatives. Many greedy upper- and middle-class citizens share with their wealthy counterparts a hatred and disdain for the poor that is so intense it borders on pathological hysteria. It has served their class interests to perpetuate the notion that the poor are mere parasites and predators. And, of course, their greed has set up a situation where many people must act in a parasitic manner in order to meet basic needs—the need for food, clothing, and shelter.

More and more it is just an accepted "fact of life" that those who are materially well off—who have more money—will have more of everything else. Hilfiker reminds us that currently "this assumption is so deeply embedded in our value system" that most everyone assumes the individual is accountable for any and all circumstance of material lack. As a consequence, "an essential principle of the free-market system, then, is actually a formulation of injustice." Hilfiker continues: "Again, few of us really believe that the world should operate this way. Some of us might agree to distribute luxuries according to wealth, but does anyone believe that food, shelter, basic education, health care, or other necessities should be distributed according to private wealth? Nonetheless, we have established a society in which even those necessities are meted out mostly on the basis of how much money people have." Unlike Hilfiker, I find many people do believe everything should be distributed according to wealth. It is not just folks with class privilege who think this way. Mass media attempts to brainwash working-class and poor people so that they, too, internalize these assumptions.

To be poor in the United States today is to be always at risk, the object of scorn and shame. Without mass-based empathy for the poor, it is possible for ruling class groups to mask class terrorism and genocidal acts. Creating and maintaining social conditions where individuals of all ages daily suffer malnutrition and starvation is a form of class warfare that increasingly goes unnoticed in this society. When huge housing projects in urban cities are torn down and the folks who dwell therein are not relocated, no one raises questions or protests. Television and newspapers provide snippets of interviews with residents saying these structures should be torn down. Of course, the public does not hear these interviewees stress the need for new public housing that is sound and affordable.

To stand in solidarity with the poor is no easy gesture at a time when individuals of all classes are encouraged to fear for their economic well-being. Certainly the fear of being taken advantage of by those in need has led many people with class privilege to turn their backs on the poor. As the gap between rich and poor intensifies in this society, those voices that urge solidarity with the poor are often drowned out by mainstream conservative voices that deride, degrade, and devalue the poor. Lack of concern for the poor is all the more possible when voices on the left ignore this reality while focusing primary attention on the machinations of the powerful. We need a concerned left politics that continues to launch powerful critique of ruling class groups even as it also addresses and attends to the issue of strategic assault and demoralization of the poor, a politics that can effectively intervene on class warfare.

Tragically, the well-off and the poor are often united in capitalist culture by their shared obsession with consumption. Oftentimes the poor are more addicted to excess because they are the most vulnerable to all the powerful messages in media and in our lives in general which suggest that the only way out of class shame is conspicuous consumption. Propaganda in advertising and in the culture as a whole assures the poor that they can be one with those who are more materially privileged if they own the same products. It helps sustain the false notion that ours is a classless society. When these values are accepted by the poor they internalize habits of being that make them act in complicity with greed and exploitation. Who has not heard materially well-off individuals talk about driving through poor neighborhoods and seeing fancy cars or massive overeating of junk food? These are the incidents the well-off emphasize to denigrate the poor while simultaneously holding them accountable for their fate.

In a culture where money is the measure of value, where it is believed that everything and everybody can be bought, it is difficult to sustain different values. Hilfiker believes: "In such a system the only way to mobilize social forces against poverty is to show how much money society would save by investing in poor neighborhoods, alternatives to prison and preventative medical care. In other words by a cost-benefit analysis of poverty." While this strategy is important, we must also face that for many people the thrill of having more is intensified by the presence of those who have less. Waste is not the issue here. To many greedy individuals, power lies in withholding resources even if it would be more economically beneficial to share.

Sharing resources is more and more looked down upon as a symptom of unnecessary guilt on the part of those who have material privilege. Individuals who wish to share resources are encouraged to think that they will be victimized by the poor. Of course, there are times when materially privileged individuals find themselves in situations where they extend help to a needy individual only to find their generosity exploited. This often leads them to denounce the poor rather than to reexamine strategies of care and support so that the most useful ones can be found. The poor are not fooled when the privileged offer castoffs and worn-out hand-me-downs as a gesture of "generosity" while buying only the new and best for themselves. This form of charity necessarily often backfires. Embedded in such seemingly "innocent" gestures are mechanisms of condescension and shaming that often assault the psyches of the poor. No doubt that is why so many poor people in our culture regard charitable gestures with suspicion. It is always possible to share resources in ways that enhance rather than devalue the humanity of the poor. It is the task of those who hold greater privilege to create practical strategies, some of which become clearer when we allow ourselves to fully empathize, to give as we would want to be given to.

To see the poor as ourselves we must want for the poor what we want for ourselves. By living simply, we all express our solidarity with the poor and our recognition that gluttonous consumption must end. Richard Foster makes a careful distinction between poverty and living simply: "Never forget that poverty is not simplicity. Poverty is a word of smaller scope. Poverty is a means of grace; simplicity is the grace itself. It is possible to get rid of things and still desire them in your heart." Confronting the endless desire that is at the heart of our individual overconsumption and global excess is the only intervention that can ward off the daily call to consume that bombards us on all sides.

Like David Hilfiker, when I told friends and colleagues that I was resigning from my academic job to focus on writing, I was warned that I was making a dangerous mistake, that I could not possibly live on an income that was between twenty and thirty thousand dollars a year. When I pointed to the reality that families of four and more live on such an income, the response would be "that's different"; the difference being, of course, one of class. The poor are expected to live with less and are socialized to accept less (badly made clothing, products, food, etc.), whereas the well-off are socialized to believe it is both a right and a necessity for us to have more, to have exactly what we want when we want it.

The call to live simply is not new news. It was a beacon light only a few years ago. And many of us embraced and remain faithful to communitarian values. Nothing threatens those values more than turning the poor into a predatory class to be both despised and feared. Covert genocidal assaults on the poor and destitute will not make the world safe for the well-to-do as many naively imagine. Better burglar alarms, more prisons, and the formation of concentration camp–like gated communities where the poor are held captive will simply reflect an everyday state of siege, of conflict and warfare, wherein the presence of any stranger, especially one who does not appear to share one's class, will incite fear and hostility. The poor know this already since they already live with the fear of being assaulted and mistreated if they are out of their place.

Solidarity with the poor is the only path that can lead our nation back to a vision of community that can effectively challenge and eliminate violence and exploitation. It invites us to embrace an ethics of compassion and sharing that will renew a spirit of loving kindness and communion that can sustain and enable us to live in harmony with the whole world.

4

Money Hungry

Everyone who grows up in a household where there is a lack of material resources knows what it feels like to want things you cannot have, to want what money can buy when there is no money to spare. Poor people know these feelings intimately. And so do individuals who are raised in homes where material resources could be available but are withheld because of avarice or domination. In patriarchal households, dominating males often withhold funds for basic necessities as a way of maintaining coercive control over wives and children. Usually, patriarchal abuse in relation to finances is talked about publicly only in relation to domestic violence. Yet there are many homes in this society where physical violence is not present wherein financial withholding by a patriarchal head of household is the accepted norm. These men do not just control the money they make, they often control the spouse's income as well. Children in these households may grow up with an extreme sense of material lack even though the financial assets of the family are more than enough to accommodate needs and desires.

In our patriarchal household, my parents believed it was the man's responsibility to provide for the family's material needs. Both my parents based their thinking about gender roles on conventional sexism. They felt the man should work outside the home and the woman should work inside the home. My father kept from my mother knowledge of how much money he made and what he did with it. He gave her a specific amount of money for household needs based not on her calculations but on what he believed was needed. When what he gave was not enough, she pleaded, cajoled, and at times begged for more.

Daddy was not a benevolent patriarch. He believed in domination and coercion. Raised in a single-parent home where there had been few pleasures and lots of hard work, he believed only in providing basic necessities. His attitudes clashed not only with the desires of his children, but also with mama's desires. While she believed it was important to work hard, she also believed it was important to have small material pleasures and delights. Whereas dad thought new school clothes and material were never needed, she understood our desire to have the occasional luxury. He rarely did. In our household there was always tension around money. That tension was rarely expressed by overt conflict between our mother and father, yet it was always there whenever we needed something that cost money.

Mama was a genius when it came to taking a small amount of money and making it go a long way. Proud to have a husband who was willing to work hard and provide for his family when we were growing up, she never complained about our father's lack of generosity. She never complained when she cooked him special food, different and more expensive than the food she ate. Yet the underlying tensions around money were always there in our household. Those tensions were most expressed by sexism, by mama's dependency on dad's income. When she no longer had small children and did the occasional work outside the home, dad simply withheld more from the household funds he gave to her.

Both our parents lived in a better economic situation than that of their family of origin. Our father knew that he had less money to spend, less control after marriage and he seemed to deeply resent the economic responsibility of children and family. Mama had never lived on her own or worked outside the home. Dependency was a norm for her. She saw it as female destiny. Being taken care of was a source of pride and traditional power. That pride was eroded over the years as our dad constantly used his financial power to control and dominate. Like many of the women sociologist Arlie Hochschild describes in *The Time Bind: When Work Becomes Home and Home Becomes Work,* working outside the home never made mama independent but it did give her a sense of self-esteem and a small amount of money to spend as she so desired.

Growing up in a large family without lots of money, I was always aware of the enormous economic burden children constituted. As young kids, when we wanted more than our household could afford, we did what most children do—whined, sulked, pleaded. But ours was a discipline-and-punish household—one in which no child could express displeasure for long. Early on we learned that if we wanted material objects beyond the basic necessities of life we could acquire them by doing odd jobs. Looking back it amazes me that when we asked mama why we could not have weekly allowances like other children we knew, she never talked about a lack of funds. She never gave voice to a sense of lack, to disappointment or anger about her family's economic fate. From her perspective we were doing well, better than most working folks with large families to feed.

Children could do odd jobs and make money. I was often "hired" by my teachers to do work around the house, to spend the night in the home of an elderly retired teacher just to be on hand in case she needed something. The money I made from these jobs, like that of my siblings, was handed over to mama. She used it to buy schoolbooks and special little things that we needed. Among us seven children, we had different responses to this arrangement. Some of us, especially my brother, resented not being able to spend money we had earned on whatever we wanted. In relation to her children our mother duplicated the manipulative use of money that our father used in relation to her.

Conflict around money was especially depressing to my psyche as a child. I was always willing to give up material desires and just accept whatever came my way. I found this a less stressful strategy than holding on to unsatisfied desire, but it was also true that unlike my siblings my major passion in life was reading, and books could be found at the library for free. I longed for pretty clothes. Instead, mama always chose for us, basing her decisions on money, whether we were getting used or new clothing. Now looking back I assume she did this to make things fit into her limited budget, but she never gave this as an explanation.

In my childhood fantasy life I was quite taken with notions of poverty and asceticism. At times I dreamed of joining a religious order. These fantasies were inspired by religious teachings but also by the fact that I just found it psychologically less stressful to give up attachment to material goods. Unlike my siblings I did not know how to ride a bicycle or play tennis, nor did I dream of playing a musical instrument or driving a car—things that cost. When I went away to college, to a world of class privilege, my material desires surfaced, again mostly around the issue of clothing. My clothes always exposed my class background; they were cheap and often garish. Sometimes I wore the expensive hand-me-downs of my classmates because it was acceptable to wear each other's clothes. The only time in my life that I ever felt like stealing was during my undergraduate years when I longed to wear beautiful clothes that were usually expensive.

My college roommate, a white girl from a working-class background, would steal things all the time. Without my knowledge, she frequently used me as her decoy. While the clerks in fancy stores were busy following the black girl around to make sure she was not stealing, the white girl was robbing them blind. We both found it difficult to be at a university filled with "rich" students (many of them were not wealthy—just upper class—but from our perspective, since nei-ther of us had any money to spare, they all seemed to be among the elect and the elite). During this period of my life I felt driven by material longings and lacks. I felt class shame around clothes. This period of my life helped me to understand my siblings better, their frustration at not being able to have material objects they longed for.

Like my mother I had a knack for making do with a little. I was always confident that any material object I desired could be found secondhand. I spent hours searching out the thrift stores where used luxuries would surface and were cheap, antique silks, cashmeres.

By age nineteen I had my own household. While we were not planning to have children early, if at all, I was ecstatic about settling down. My partner was content to let me take care of household stuff. And while we split household labor in perfect feminist fashion, decor and furnishing were mainly my domain.

Also from a working-class background, my partner had been raised in a single-parent home, in apartments. I had never known anyone who lived in an apartment growing up. In our small town almost everybody lived in houses. When the first projects were built, they were built like little duplexes, not like the apartments that would come later. To me it was vital to have a home, to make it the sanctu-ary you want it to be. My partner did not have any interest in home-making.

Living together as students, our budget was limited. We did not see ourselves as working class. We saw ourselves more as bohemians who were beyond class. We were not into buying new things or trying to get rich; we just wanted to read, write, eat good food, and indulge in passions like buying books, records, and, in my case, clothes. The first real debt I incurred in my life beyond my school loans was for clothes. Tired of never having enough money, I decided to look for a serious job, and that meant I needed serious clothing. With a credit card given me when I was a student, I swiftly amassed a clothing debt I could not afford to pay. In the household of my growing up, getting into debt had always spelled the beginning of financial ruin. When the creditors and bill collectors started calling, I felt more stressed about money than I had ever felt in my life and more ashamed.

My partner had no sense of shame. Time and time again, he told me "debt is the American way of life." He did not allow himself to be stressed about money. If he had money, he spent it quickly and freely. I agonized about the way money was spent. Like me, he had come from a family where money was hard to come by. His mother was punitive about money, especially spending for pleasure. He recalled having to sneak records into their home so she would not become enraged that he was spending hard-earned money on nonsense. Rebelling against his home training, he spent money recklessly. We fought about money. And I was not surprised when I read somewhere that quarrels over money were one of the primary reasons couples split up.

Our quarrels about money reached an all-time high when I wanted us to buy a house. Since I had screwed up my credit record, he needed to acquire the loan on his own. He did not want the financial burden but ultimately consented to keep the peace. Obsessed with the desire never to be out of control financially again, I read all the books I could find on managing money. I learned how to keep a budget. I learned that if you put money into a savings account you could not keep taking it out whenever you needed something extra—you had to leave it and forget about it. When I came up with a plan for our financial situation where we would have a household account, putting in an agreed-upon amount of money monthly to cover all expenses then having our separate checking accounts, we stopped fighting about money.

Like many women who had followed the men in their lives to the places where they had work, I was always looking for work and trying to finish university so I could get better work. I never made as much money as the man I lived with, even when I did the same amount of work. If I taught three classes as a lecturer, I made a mere fraction of what he made teaching three classes as a professor. Rather than trying to work out a financial plan based on money earned, we combined money earned and time spent in labor, deciding on equitable contributions based on that. This meant he always contributed more because he made more. Yet it was also true that I spent a disproportionate amount of my income on the household.

I often worked long hours for little pay and was usually miserable. My partner often encouraged me to quit working and work at home to become the writer I wanted to be. I was too afraid of becoming economically dependent on a man to stop working. My father's use of money as a tool of patriarchal power had instilled in me a fear of depending on any man. In truth my partner was not like dad when it came to issues of money, but I was still too afraid to stop working. My involvement with feminist thinking reinforced the importance of economic self-sufficiency.

While working gave me a sense of my own agency, I did not make enough money to keep myself in the manner to which I was accustomed. And when I separated from my partner of more than twelve years, like so many women, I suffered a major drop in income. My lifestyle changed drastically. I was in my mid-thirties, with school debts that were more than thirty thousand dollars. I could not afford to stay in the area we lived in, as there were no jobs for me, nor could I keep the house. Finishing my doctorate, I took a job teaching in New Haven at Yale University, where salaries for assistant professors were notoriously low and the cost of living high.

When I took stock of my finances after the separation, I was upset with myself. Even though I had always worked, I still had structured my life on the assumption that I would be in the relationship forever, my income bolstered by his as his was by mine. And all the more so because while he made more money, he also recklessly spent more. Despite all my knowledge of and commitment to feminist thinking, I found myself in the same economic place as that of many adult women who have spent ten years or more in a committed partnership with a man. My debts were many and my income was not great. It was psychologically demoralizing not to be able to keep myself in the manner to which I had been accustomed.

During these years at my first tenure track teaching job, my sole concern was paying off my debts. Coming to teach at an Ivy League institution where most students and professors come from privileged-class backgrounds brought me face to face with class issues that were not that different from those that had surfaced when I was an under-graduate and leaving home for the first time. Assistant professors often joked about not standing behind any of our students at the bank machine because it was just too depressing to see that they had more money. While this, no doubt, was true, it was equally true that many professors who lived on what they considered to be low wages had incomes that were supplemented by family money, or they hoped to inherit incomes from family at some point. Like many indivi-duals from working-class backgrounds who enter the ranks of the privileged, I was unfamiliar with the workings of trust funds and inheritances. Yale was the place where I first heard discussions of these matters.

Financially naive, like many folks from poor and working-class backgrounds, I had never thought about the role of trust funds and inheritances. Debt was all I could imagine inheriting from my family. Discussions of class surfaced primarily in relation to spending money. Realizing that I owed more money than I had ever made in income depressed me. The fact that I was thirty-something and had no more money than when I was in my twenties added to that depression. All I desired was to pay my debts and save money. Unlike many of my peers I did not live beyond my means. As in undergraduate school, my colleagues spent huge sums of money on fancy eating and drink-ing. When I refused to indulge, I was teased. Unlike my undergradu-ate years where my financial situation often caused me embarrass-ment and now and then shame, I was not bothered. I knew that my class position was different from theirs and that I could not pretend to be like them, or share their attitudes about money. It caused me greater distress to confront the reality that my class position was now different from my parents', yet my life was filled with the same underlying stress about money that had characterized our household. The desire to eliminate this stress led me to learn how to spend money wisely. In my mid-thirties, clothes continued to be the material objects which sometimes led me to overspend. In general, I was not a big spender. My flat resembled all the places I had lived in as a student. Still I was not tempted to live beyond my means, to live in a better place, because I wanted to be free of debt, to be free of the stress caused by financial worry.

This period of my life made me cautious about spending money. I felt a constant need to be frugal. Since I did not fit in so many ways at Yale, I did not expect to be awarded tenure despite excellent teaching and publications. Instead, I searched for another job. Hired by Oberlin College to teach a full course load on a one-semester basis for a reasonable salary, I finally had an academic arrangement suited to my first vocation—the desire to write. Unlike New Haven, the small town of Oberlin was a place where rents were reasonable and the cost of living low. I rented a house owned by the college and created a lifestyle that was more middle class. I bought nice furniture, art, and fancy dishes and made a home for myself. Even though years had passed since I had left my longtime companion, when I found a small old house to buy in Oberlin he bought my share of our previous place, thus providing me with the means to purchase a home for myself.

Most professors in the small town of Oberlin bought big houses, beautiful Victorians or fancy new places. All my life I had dreams of one day buying a rambling old house that would be full of books and wonderful treasures. Yet when faced with carrying financial burdens alone I took all the money I had and bought a little house with cash, a house I could afford, a modest place. Buying this place kept me free of debt. It was not the house of my dreams but it was a comfortable dwelling that allowed me to pursue my most passionate dream of becoming a full-time writer.

I had read somewhere that only two percent of artists in our society are able to make a living from their work. Most of the writers I knew were trying to get teaching jobs so that they could be more secure. My teaching job at Oberlin did not pay a huge salary. Indeed, my income did not change significantly when I moved from New Haven to Oberlin, but the cost of living was significantly lower.

During my Oberlin years I wrote more books and became more engaged with Buddhist thought and practice. I liked combining liberatory narratives from Christian teachings with Buddhism. In both cases, living simply and sharing resources with others was a basic tenet of spiritual faith and action. Living simply did not mean a life without luxuries; it meant a life without excess. I had always wanted to have a sturdy fancy car and bought one for my fortieth birthday. In keeping with the practice of living simply, I bought an expensive used car which was still much cheaper than a new model.

Before I purchased this car, I drove a Volkswagen for years. I had no difficulty letting others who were in need borrow my car. This gesture was in keeping with my recognition of interdependency and commitment to sharing resources. However, once I bought a fancy car I found myself being less generous. Even minor repairs on this car cost lots of money. The one time I loaned it to a friend, it was returned needing repairs. Suddenly, I found myself more attached to this material object and also more protective of it. This was my first experience of owning a material object where identification with the object altered my relationships to others. It helped me to understand the fear on the part of those with greater class privilege that they or their objects will be damaged if they share resources.

Acquiring costly objects, whether those that fill functional needs or those that are pure luxury items, has been the experience that has most brought me face to face with my own capacity for selfishness and greed. During the many years of my life when I made less and had few, if any, costly objects, I was always willing to be generous. The more money I made and the more objects I acquired, the more I was tempted to move away from the spirit of generosity and the closer I came to being seduced by greed. That greedy voice tells you things like you don't owe other people anything; you've worked hard to get your stuff, they should work hard; or you've earned it, you have a right to spend it on whatever you want. I was shocked that such thoughts would even enter my head.

I felt I was falling into the trap many individuals from poor and working-class backgrounds fall into when we move into more privileged class positions. Constant vigilance (that includes a principled practice of sharing my resources) has been the only stance that keeps me from falling into the hedonistic consumerism that so quickly can lead individuals with class privilege to live beyond their means and therefore to feel they are in a constant state of "lack," thus having no reason to identify with those less fortunate or to be accountable for improving their lot. Time and time again, I hear individuals who make a lot of money but spend way beyond what they earn speak of themselves as though they are poor and needy. They do not see themselves as victims of the culture of greed that hedonistic consumerism produces. Yet this faulty logic lies at the heart of their inability to recognize the suffering of those who are truly in need.

We all know that constant craving can produce an endless sense of lack even in the face of plenty. When people are materially privileged and can satisfy cravings at will, greed has no limits. At a time in my life when my income began to soar way beyond any amount that I had ever imagined, I observed how swiftly I began to fall prey to greedy thoughts and longings. This observation was a crucial one because I have spent so much of my life feeling proud of myself for not being a victim of hedonistic consumerism. Experiencing how easy it is to be seduced by material longings enabled me to be empathic toward folks who do fall prey to the vicissitudes of greed, especially individuals who have lived most of their lives in economic circumstances that have never allowed them to indulge material desire.

Seeing that the tendency to fall prey to greed lies within myself and everyone else keeps me from feeling self-righteous. Many people who would never express greediness by hedonistic consumerism do so by hoarding. They derive a feeling of power over others, especially those who lack material privilege, simply by knowing that they have reserves stored away. These individuals may often live simply or even take on the mantle of poverty, but they are addicted to making and hoarding money. And they are as attached and identified with material resources as those individuals who express their greediness by flaunting excessive wealth and privilege. Money is their god even though they may never worship it in a manner that is visible to others.

While my parents did not discuss money matters openly when we were growing up, most of the poor and working-class folks in our neighborhood talked freely about money. Everyone talked about how much things cost. When I entered worlds where individuals were materially privileged, now and then I would ask about the cost of material objects they purchased, and again I would be told by someone, who would take me aside, that it was not polite to talk about how much things cost. This censoring of public discussions of money was not simply a matter of polite social decorum, it deflected attention from underlying competition about money. It allows those who have more to conceal their fortunes from others. It sets up the condition where individuals can feel no economic accountability to others. Most importantly, it enables those who have class privilege and know how to use money in a manner that is beneficial to hoard this knowledge.

In my transition from the working class to the ranks of the upper-middle class, I was continually amazed by my lack of understanding about the way money works in this society. Simple information about interest-producing savings accounts and certainly all knowledge of investment possibilities were not known to me. And if you do not know something exists, you do not know to ask about it. It was only when I began to read books about money that I learned the importance of making a budget. Many poor and working-class people think that because they have so little resources available, it is not important to make budgets. From books, I learned that it is important.

Michael Phillips' book *The Seven Laws of Money* was particularly helpful. Written from a quirky perspective, his was one of the rare books about making money that emphasized the importance of doing work that one cares deeply about. It did not negate the notion that one could be a writer, an artist, and be economically self-sufficient. That was important to me since the ultimate goal of my working life was to reach a point where I would not need to teach to make a living but could concentrate on writing.

Understanding the class politics of money and greed has been essential to creating a life where I can be economically self-sufficient without hoarding and without refusing to identify with those who remain economically disadvantaged. Morally and ethically, it is important for me to acknowledge my capacity to be greedy so that I do not indulge in a form of spiritual materialism where I see myself as superior to, better than, and more deserving of a good life than those who are daily consumed by greedy longings. Ostentatious materiality, the flaunting of excess, erodes community no matter whether it is done by the greedy rich or the suffering poor. I have always felt a greater sympathy toward individuals who live most of their lives without material privilege indulging in ostentatious displays of material excess than those who have always been materially well off. Yet I know that if we are to live in a world where sharing of resources is a norm, everyone—the poor and the well-to-do—must resist overidentification with material objects. That resistance challenges and changes the culture of greed.

5

The Politics of Greed

Being overwhelmed by greed is a state of mind and being that most human beings have experienced at some time in our lives. Most children experience greed in relation to food—endless longing for sweets, longings that lead to hoarding, stealing, or some combination of these. Excessive indulgence in favorite foods, especially sweet ones, by children often leads to sickness. Consequently, many of us learn while quite young that greed has its dangers, that it causes suffering. Most children are taught that excessive desire is bad. Parents, even dysfunctional ones, do not wish to raise a child to be greedy.

These childhood imprints lose power in today's hedonistic consumer culture where the good life has come to be seen as the life where one can have whatever one wants, where no desire is seen as excessive. Beyond childhood squabbles over toys or food where greedy desires to possess and hoard surfaced sometimes, for most folks, religious teachings were the only other place where greed was talked about, where it was deemed sinful and dangerous. The decline of substantive religious practice in contemporary everyday life engendered in part by the worship of technological advancement and our ongoing cultural obsession with progress has practically eliminated any concern with the ethics of greed.

Indeed, as a nation where the culture of narcissism reigns supreme, where I, me, and mine are all that matters, greed becomes the order of the day. While the sixties and seventies can be characterized as a time in the nation when there was a widespread sense of bounty that could be shared precisely because excess was frowned upon, the eighties and nineties are the years where fear of scarcity increased even as a culture of hedonistic excess began to fully emerge. Widespread communal concern for justice and social welfare was swiftly replaced by conservative notions of individual accountability and self-centered materialism. Zillah Eisenstein notes in *Global Obscenities*: "The extremes of wealth and poverty within the united states also mirror the extremes across the globe. The wealthiest 20 percent of u.s. citizens received 99 percent of the total gain in marketable wealth between 1983 and 1989. More than 38 million people live in poverty in the united states, of whom more than 40 percent are under eighteen years of age." The rich are getting richer and the poor poorer.

Radical young politicos from privileged backgrounds who had sought to intervene on oppressive capitalism became adults who were eager to find and keep their place in the existing economic system. And if this system was fast turning our nation into a world of haves and have-nots with little in between, they wanted to remain in the ranks of the privileged. Once they advocated living simply and sharing resources, now they join their more conservative counterparts in embracing and advocating individual gain over communal good. Together both groups put in place a system of protectionism to further support and perpetuate their diverse class interests.

Since the radicals and/or liberals who had once repudiated class privilege brought to their reclaiming of class power a more open view toward the masses than their ancestors, they were quite willing to let go of old notions, whether rooted in racism or sexism, to exploit the material desires of any group. More than any other group in the nation's history, this group was and is willing to forego allegiance to race or gender to promote their class interests. If they could make a fortune promoting and selling a product to any group, they were willing to play and prey upon any need or vulnerability that would aid in their accumulation of wealth. Suddenly, spheres of advertising that had always excluded poor and lower-class people had no trouble mining their culture, their images, if it would lead to profit. A new generation of upper and ruling classes had come of age. They were motivated more by the desire for ever-increasing profit than by sustained allegiance to race or gender.

These newly converted fiscal conservatives were different from the generations who preceded them precisely because they had crossed the tracks, so to speak, in that they had not only lived outside the mores of their class of origin, they had a more realistic and experiential understanding of less-privileged groups. While they understood their needs, they also understood their longings. Anyone who spends time with people who are underprivileged and poor knows how much of their energies are spent longing for material goods, not just for the basic necessities of life, but also for luxuries. It is no accident that just as the gap between classes in this nation began to widen as never before, the notion that this is a classless society, where anyone can make it big irrespective of their origins, gained greater currency in the public imagination.

Opportunities for class mobility created by radical political movements for social justice, civil rights, and women's liberation, especially in the workforce, meant that there were individuals who could serve as examples of the popular truism that "anyone can make it big in America." Multimass media has played the central role as the propagandistic voice promoting the notion that this culture remains a place of endless opportunity, where those on the bottom can reach the top. In the areas of sports and entertainment, more and more individual black stars were entering the ranks of the rich. Ironically, the token presence of individual white women and people of color among the rich and powerful was effectively used to validate the existing social and economic structure by conservatives who had religiously fought to keep them out. By the early eighties the idea that sexism and racism had been eradicated, coupled with the assumption that the existing white supremacist capitalist patriarchy could work for everybody gained momentum and with it the notion that those groups for whom it did not work were at fault.

Along with the revamped myth that everyone who worked hard could rise from the bottom of our nation's class hierarchy to the top was the insistence that the old notions of oppressor class and oppressed class were no longer meaningful, because when it came to the issue of material longing, the poor, working, and middle classes desired the same things that the rich desired, including the desire to exercise power over others. What better proof of this could there be than calling attention to the reality that individuals from marginal groups who had been left out of the spheres of class power entered these arenas and conducted themselves in the same manner as the established groups—"the good old boys." Once the public could be duped into thinking that the gates of class power and privilege were truly opened for everyone, then there was no longer a need for an emphasis on communalism or sharing resources, for ongoing focus on social justice.

More importantly, there was ample evidence among token marginal individuals who entered the ranks of ruling class privilege that they, like their mainstream counterparts, could be bought—could and would succumb to the corrupting temptations of greed. The way had been paved to bring to the masses the message that excess was acceptable. Greed was the order of the day, and to make a profit by any means necessary was merely to live out to the fullest degree the American work ethic.

In relation to the poor and underclass, this permission to indulge in excess fostered and perpetuated the infiltration into previously stable communities, especially black communities, a predatory capitalist-based drug culture that would bring money for luxuries to a few, a symbolic ruling class. Suddenly-impoverished communities where life had been hard but safe were turned into war zones. Greed for material luxuries, whether a pair of expensive sneakers, a leather jacket, or a brand-new car, led individuals to prey upon the pain of their neighbors and sell drugs. Many a family starts out disapproving of drug culture but suffers a change of heart when money earned in that enterprise pays bills, buys necessities, and provides luxuries.

Those who suffer the weight of this greed-based predatory capitalism are the addicted. Robbed of the capacity to function as citizens of any community (unable to work, to commune with others, even to eat), they become the dehumanized victims of an ongoing protracted genocide. Unlike the drugs used in the past, like marijuana and heroin, drugs like cocaine and crack/cocaine disturbed the mental health of the addicted and created in them cravings so great that no moral or ethical logic could intervene to stop immoral behavior.

All of us who have lived or live in poor communities know that the addicts in these neighborhoods do not prey upon the rich. They steal from family and neighbors. They exploit and violate the people they know most intimately. Since addiction is not about relatedness, they destroy the affectional bonds that once mediated the hardships of poverty and lack. Contemporary street drug enterprises sanctioned by the government (if they were not, law enforcement would rid our streets of drugs perhaps using some of the millions that go to support the military industrial complex) have done more to promote and perpetuate a culture of greed among the poor than even the propagandistic mass media, which encourages endless consumption.

Drug trafficking is the only economic enterprise that enables a poor person to acquire the means to drive the same cars and wear the same clothes as the rich. Of course, unlike the legitimized beneficiaries of greedy capitalism, these profiteers lack the power to influence government spending or public policy. They function only as a fascist force that brings violence and devastation into what were once stable communities. They do the work of exploitation and genocide for the white supremacist capitalist patriarchal ruling class. Like mercenaries sent from first world nations to small countries around the world, they devastate and destabilize. This is class warfare. Yet the media deflects attention away from class politics and focuses instead on drug culture and youth violence as if no connection exists between this capitalist exploitation and the imperialist economies that are wreaking havoc on the planet.

Mass media, especially the world of advertising, pimps the values of the ruling class to all other groups. A strong organized politicized working class does not exist in the United States today precisely because, through the socialization of mass media, a vast majority of poor and working-class people, along with their middle-class counterparts, learn to think ideologically like the rich even when their economic circumstance would suggest otherwise. This has been made glaringly evident by the response of the public to efforts to end welfare. Lecturing around the country to groups of working people, including black folks, I am amazed when individuals who should know better talk about welfare recipients as lazy predators who do not want to work. Eisenstein contends: "Ending welfare as the united states has known it also kills the idea that we share a public responsibility for one another. The extreme forms of this new poverty constitute the other side of the process of privatization begun a quarter century ago." The folks who wanted to end welfare had little knowledge of the actual dollar amounts spent.

None of these people were willing to look critically at unemployment in this society. They could not let go of their misguided assumptions that jobs are endlessly and always available. Not even the economic crisis that is sorely impacting on their lives at home and at work alerts them to the realities of predatory capitalism. Their lack of sympathy for the poor unites them ideologically with greedy people of means who only have contempt for the poor. Once the poor can be represented as totally corrupt, as being always and only morally bankrupt, it is possible for those with class privilege to eschew any responsibility for poverty and the suffering it generates.

Greed is the attribute the poor often share with the well-to-do that lends credence to negative stereotypes, which imply that were the poor empowered, they would hold power and exploit in the same manner as the more privileged classes do. Certainly, it is probably true that the greedy poor are unlikely to act in ways more ethical and moral than the greedy rich. Hence the need in mainstream culture to socialize more and more people of all classes, especially the poor, to see greed as essential to making it in this society, as necessary for survival. If at one time individuals were convinced that it's a dog-eat-dog world and only the strong survive, now the message is that survival belongs only to the greedy.

Greed has become the common bond shared by many of the poor and well-to-do. When honest caring citizens, especially our political leaders, are corrupted by longings for fame, wealth, and power, it demoralizes everyone who wants justice for all. Hopelessness generates inactivity. It is not easy to ward off the seductive temptations calling to everyone daily in a culture of excess. Constant vigilance is required to sustain integrity. None of us are exempt. The possibility of greed taking hold in all our psyches is ever present. It can be and often is the oppressor within. Confronting this reality without fear or shame is the only way we garner the moral strength to confront and overcome temptation and corruption.

6

Being Rich

Speaking openly about money remains taboo in polite society. I never meet wealthy people who speak about themselves as "rich." More often than not people of means display their wealth and the status it gives them through material objects—where they live, shop, what they own. While they may not speak openly about money, many wealthy individuals think about their riches all the time. Possessing wealth in a greedy culture, where millions of poor people live without the basic necessities of life, they work to hold on to what they have, using it to make more. Protecting their class interests takes time. Many wealthy people live in fear that the people they meet want to get money from them and, as a consequence, thinking about money often dominates their personal relationships.

Most individuals from poor and working-class backgrounds do not work directly as servants for the rich and know no wealthy people. Even though citizens of this nation like to insist that the United States is a classless society, we all know that the rich live apart from the rest of us and that they live differently. Growing up in the fifties, I was surrounded by folks who wanted to have more money to buy the things in life their hearts desired. I was most moved by the longings of grown women who worked hard keeping household, doing jobs outside the home, raising children while caring for the needs and whims of dominating men. Their longing for a nice house and appliances that worked made sense to me. While they talked about these longings, they did not sit around hoping to be rich.

In our communities we were schooled by religious thought to believe that wealth was dangerous. We learned from the Bible that it was hard for the rich to enter heaven because being rich made one more susceptible to greed, to hoarding. In the working-class and poor neighborhoods of my upbringing, most folks believed that one could not be rich without exploiting others. While it was fine to long for more money to live well, it was considered a waste of time and energy to long to be rich. In this world we did not identify with the rich or share their values. On a more basic level we simply assumed the rich were the enemy of working people.

More than any other media, television fundamentally altered the attitudes of poor and working-class people, as well as those of more privileged classes, toward the rich. Largely through marketing and advertising, television promoted the myth of the classless society, offering on one hand images of an American dream fulfilled wherein any and everyone can become rich and on the other suggesting that the lived experience of this lack of class hierarchy was expressed by our equal right to purchase anything we could afford. The rich came to be represented as heroic. By championing hedonistic consumerism and encouraging individuals of all classes to believe that ownership of a particular object mediated the realities of class, mass media created a new image of the rich.

On television and in magazines, the rich were and are fictively depicted as caring and generous toward impoverished classes. They are portrayed as eager to cross class boundaries and hang with diverse groups of people. Unlike the "undeserving" poor or the "unenlightened" middle classes, these images tell that the wealthy do not long to just stay with folks like themselves, that the rich are open, kind, vulnerable. And more importantly that they "suffer" as much as anyone else. Daytime and nighttime soap operas depict the lives of the rich as one sad crisis after another. On television screens, the vast majority of rich people work long hours. While they may have servants, they labor alongside them.

These images served and serve to whitewash the reality that the rich are primarily concerned with promoting their class interests, even when to do so they must exploit others. On the screen the rich are too busy coping with their own pain to inflict pain on others. And indeed most of television constructs a false image of a classless society since the vast majority of images depicted suggest most people are well-to-do, if not rich, or already on their way to becoming rich. Mass media lets us know that the rich are like everybody else in that they live to consume. Hence, it is through consumerism that the evils of class difference are transcended. In *Global Obscenities,* Zillah Eisenstein explains how this works: "Consumer culture and consumerism are woven through a notion of individualism that seduces everyone, the haves and have-nots alike. Consumerism is equated with individual freedom. Transnational media representations construct consumerist culture as democratic—open, free, where anything is possible. Its underbelly—poverty, hunger, and unemployment—remain uninteresting to mainstream media." Mass media never celebrates the lives of those who live simply, never acknowledges in a celebratory way the poor and underprivileged who live happy, meaningful lives.

By the eighties the only image of the poor we were likely to see on our television screens came on cop shows or the occasional hospital drama. Usually when they appear the poor are demonized. They are self-centered, corrupt, and dysfunctional. Depicted as liars and schemers, they are usually criminals. On television the working class are allowed to be funny now and then. *Roseanne,* a show that portrayed the white working class in a complex way, stayed on the air for a long time. Yet its popularity could not be sustained in a world where no one really wants to be identified as working class.

Frank's Place offered progressive images of the working class, especially black people, but though enjoyed widely by audiences it did not have a long shelf life. Producers and viewers tend to keep on the air programs with negative depictions of the working class, which show them to be petty, unkind, xenophobic, and racist toward any group unlike themselves.

Nowadays, where sitcoms of the working class used to appear on our screens, a range of shows featuring upper-middle-class young people abound. On these shows, identification with wealth and privilege is depicted as a norm. The fact that the television well-to-do are in their late twenties and early thirties strengthens the myth that anybody who works hard can make it. None of these shows reflect any aspect of the growing class divisions in our society. By the end of the eighties, images of working-class and poor people appeared on television screens primarily in cop shows. Depicted as lacking in morals, as criminals, as without humanizing affection, these images promote disdain for the underprivileged and identification with the privileged.

The rise in television talk shows and tabloid journalism furthered identification with the rich more so than fictional dramas. Real life "rich" people, usually celebrities, appear on these programs and talk about their lives—their problems. Watching these shows, viewers are not only able to imagine that they can rise to fame and fortune, they can have a sense of intimacy with the rich, which belies the reality that they have little or no contact with rich people in their daily lives.

Television is not the only mass media "selling" the notion that identification with the rich and powerful is the only way to get ahead in this society; magazines and newspapers exploit the fascination underprivileged people have for the lives of the rich and famous. No recent event in the nation's history dramatized as graphically the extent to which a mass audience of people identify with the rich as much as public reaction to Princess Diana's tragic death. Of course, national fixation with her life and her fate was rarely talked about in mass media as tied to an obsession with class hierarchy. It was much easier to portray public fascination and grief for Princess Diana as tied to the fact that she was not from a ruling class background. Of course, the fact that she was from an upper-class background was obscured, and hers became a rags-to-riches story. Such stories capture the imagination of an American public that does not want to let go of the myth of a classless society where all can rise. By identifying with Princess Diana they could not only reaffirm the rags-to-riches fantasy but also indulge their fantasies of being rich and famous.

Despite Diana's tragic fate, the notion that wealth and privilege bring happiness continues to dominate the consciousness of many people, especially the poor and working class. Public narratives where individual rich people share the tragic elements of their lives do nothing to change public opinion that wealth brings happiness. Since the mass public rarely sees the rich up close and personal in daily life, fantasy can always overshadow reality. A recent spread in the *New York Times* magazine section on the issue of "status" conveniently ignores the ever-widening gap between the rich and the poor in an effort to foster the false impression that anyone can reside at the top of our nation's class hierarchy. On the front page, the first editorial cited was titled "In a Class-Free Society." All the articles address the headlined issue: "What We Look Up To Now: The Democratization of Status in America."

No one knows better than the rich the truth of class difference. Protecting their class interests so that the poor and working class do not engage in any form of class warfare that would undermine or in any way destabilize their comfort, wealthy people often covertly spend more time thinking about class and money than any other group. Yet they remain reluctant to talk openly about their wealth, especially with individuals who do not share their class backgrounds.

Many rich people find it easier to avoid questions of class in relationships by choosing to forge bonds solely within their own class. Rich people I know or have known are much more willing to talk about the way in which wealth and the privileges that come with it estrange and alienate them rather than speaking of the power it brings. Whenever they are relating to people who are not materially privileged, they fear that the attraction is their privilege and not who they are. Individuals who inherited wealth as children and who have never worked at a paying job often feel they must mask their class privilege. They, like many of their wealthy peers, live in fear of being exploited and/or harassed by those in need.

While most rich folks protect their class interests by preying upon the poor and needy, they tend to deflect from this reality by projecting an image of themselves as constantly preyed upon by needy predators. Even wealthy people who see themselves as politically progressive and willing to aid others project an image of themselves as vulnerable, in need of protection from the greedy masses. The greed of the rich is often denied. Lots of rich people imagine that living in a miserly way means that they are not attached to wealth, that they are not greedy.

A rich acquaintance boasted about her reluctance to buy anything new. She wore her clothes until they were tattered and worn. Even then she did not discard them. She bundled them up to give to the "needy." Growing up I can vividly recall black women who worked as maids in the homes of well-off white people expressing their contempt for employers who would give them worn and sometimes soiled raggedy items. Their rich employers expose their greed by their hoarding, their miserly habits. And it is a greed that fuels their contempt for the needy. Since they "get by on a little," they assume everyone else not only can but should. It is quite different to take on the posture of asceticism when one has riches stashed away than to live in a state of lack where there is no hope of ever having access to material plenty.

Now and then progressive individuals who are rich grapple with the question of how they can best use their resources to empower the largest number of folks, especially those who lack resources. Yet these individuals are rare. Most people, whether they are born wealthy, inherit wealth, or achieve it through hard work and luck, focus more

on what they must do to maintain and increase their wealth. A number of "rich" individuals I interviewed emphatically expressed that
they did not see themselves as rich. They would point to friends and
colleagues who have billions. In all cases, they judged their class status
by those who had more rather than those who had less.

This attitude surfaces among all classes in this society. Again and
again I hear individuals with varying degrees of class privilege speaking of themselves as though they are suffering lack because they per-
ceive others as having so much more. Mass media has fostered this
sense of lack in both those who have abundant privilege and those
who have little. If privileged people feel "lack," there is no reason they
should feel accountable to those who are truly needy. In the fifties,
many working-class and middle-class families reminded children of
the starving on the planet when we were reluctant to eat or constantly complaining about our lot. Then, being wasteful was perceived as an act of aggression against those who had nothing. When I
was little, I thought that these starving masses were mere fictions created by worried parental imaginations. It was a shock to later face the
truth that not only did they exist, but that this country's wasteful use
of a huge portion of the world's resources did and does create conditions of deprivation globally. Daily, children in the United States are
shocked to learn that thousands of children are starving to death not
only elsewhere in the world but here in our nation as well.

The rich are able to make notions of unlimited growth and expan-
sion work for them economically. The throwaway culture of planned
obsolescence that this mode of thinking and being has produced,
while useful to the rich, has utterly undermined the class power of
middle-class, working-class, and poor people. Wanting and wasting are
practices that keep the have-nots from utilizing their limited material
resources in the most life-enhancing and productive ways. Since the
vast majority of these folks imagine that the rich are indulging every
desire (since that is what mass media tells them) they have no under-

standing of the ways in which the rich use their resources to produce more resources for themselves.

Not only do the vast majority of the rich keep their knowledge of basic economic skills from the poor, they invest in all forms of cultural production that encourage endless consumption on the part of those who have class privilege. As individuals without class privilege come to believe that they can assume an equal standing with those who are rich and powerful by consuming the same objects, they ally themselves with the class interests of the rich and collude in their own exploitation. Mass media has been the pedagogical tool used to teach the poor and working class to think like the rich. Ideologically, through mass media seduction, many of the world's have-nots take on the thoughts and values of ruling classes. In everyday life they ideologically join with the rich to protect the class interests of the wealthy.

Socialized by the media to believe that ruling classes are morally better and superior to those without class privilege, they do not feel allegiance to members of their own class or to those who are less fortunate. They believe that the wealthy have earned their right to rule. And as a consequence they abandon any political commitment to economic justice or to ethical values that condemn greed and exploitation. While it is true that more than ever before in our nation's history rare individuals of any creed or color can enter the portals of the rich, they cannot maintain this class position and class power without betraying the interests of those who are needy. I interviewed one of the richest men in this society and asked him what he liked most about his wealth. He boldly replied that what he liked most about his shift from the middle-class to the ruling wealthy elite was the power over others it gave to him, that he could make them do things they would ordinarily not do. His candor was unusual. Most ruling class individuals mask their pleasure in domination and exploitation.

Traditional Christian teaching about the wealthy condemned greed. The apostle Paul declared that those who desire wealth have "pierced their heart with many pangs" (Timothy 6:9-10). Biblical teachings suggest that the rich must work harder for grace because they will be sorely tempted to exploit and hoard their wealth rather than be guided by the spiritual commandments admonishing them to share. The disciples were puzzled when Jesus explained to them that a camel could slip through the eye of a needle with greater ease than the rich could enter the kingdom of God. They were puzzled because prior to hearing this message they simply assumed that prosperity was a sign of being among God's chosen elect. They were astounded to learn that the poor had greater standing in the eyes of the divine than the rich. Then they were taught that it was not sinful to be rich; it was sinful to become attached to wealth, to be avaricious and hardhearted.

Nowadays much new age spirituality attempts to undermine traditional biblical condemnation of the greedy rich by insisting that those who prosper are the chosen, the spiritual elect. But there is a great difference between celebrating prosperity and the pursuit of unlimited wealth. Traditional religious thought was correct in its insistence that it is difficult and dangerous to be among the wealthy. To be wealthy and remain committed to justice is no easy task. We hear little from the wealthy who use their means to further the cause of justice, of economic self-sufficiency for all. Despite their good deeds, this silence maintains their class solidarity with those who exploit and oppress, as they are best situated to challenge their peers, to offer new ways of thinking and being in the world.

Ruling class groups keep themselves separate so that the masses cannot know who they are and how they really live. Most importantly, separation allows them to live the fantasy that there is no connection between their opulent lifestyles and the misery these lifestyles produce. They live in states of denial and deflect attention away from the imperialist violence enacted in their name globally to protect their class interests. However, they have no difficulty asserting the fascist thought and action needed to protect their wealth when they feel threatened. It is this link that makes their ruthless allegiance to a class hierarchy where they are on top a danger to us all.

Prosperity enhances life. As a nation we should uphold the belief that everyone has the right to a life of well-being, which includes access to prosperity. The rare rich folk who use their resources to enhance their lives and the well-being of the communities in which they live exemplify that possessing wealth is not an evil. Wealth built and maintained by the exploitation and oppression of others undermines a democratic vision of prosperity. When we recognize that abundance can be spread around, that more of our nation's citizens should have access to material plenty that enables us all to live "a good life," the rich will not need to live in constant fear and alienation. And those with little or no class privilege will not be preyed upon by the greedy.

7

The Me-Me Class:
The Young and the
Ruthless

The notion that everyone can be wealthy has supplanted the idea of the United States as a classless society. Indeed, the fantasy that cuts across class is the dream of a world where everyone can be wanton and wasteful as they consume the world's riches. Endless indulgence of a fantasy life used to be solely the cultural terrain of rich white men. More than any other group they had the power to realize dreams and fantasies. Advertising changed all that. Through the manipulation of images, it constructs a fictive United States where everyone has access to everything. And no one, no matter their politics or values, can easily remain untouched by these insistent narratives of unlimited plenty posthypnotically telling us we are what we possess.

Hypervigilant individuals can turn off our television sets but we walk and drive in a world crowded with advertising. Whenever we seek to purchase any item in our lives we enter the world of advertised images. In recent years, we open bills for basic necessities like water, electricity, or credit cards where the envelopes are now designed to push products. This makes it practically impossible to ignore mass media images that push the fiction that there are unlimited resources and unlimited access.

Teenagers are the largest growth population. Studies already show that their favorite activity is shopping and that they spend on the average more than twenty dollars a day consuming. Greater economic success for privileged parents coupled with societal support of hedonistic consumerism has produced a new generation of young people who see no value in hard work but who believe that value lies in status, and power lies in getting one's needs met, especially material needs.

Today's youth culture is centered around consumption. Whether it's wearing designer clothes or cruising in luxury cars, materialism becomes the basis of all transactions. For young people, the world is their marketplace. All one's worth, mass media advertising tells them, is determined by material things. Ironically, such thinking produces a symbolically "classless" society in that these values are shared by youth culture irrespective of race, gender, or class positionality. While today's youth are eager to live in a world where racism does not exist, they do not want to do the political work of changing themselves or society. That world entails confronting pain and hostility. And they are the generations who are constantly told via mass media that only losers feel pain, that the good life is a life without difficulties. They are constantly told that the only peace and happiness they can have will come to them through rugged individualism, through a focus on meeting self-centered needs. In a world where pathological narcissism is the order of the day, it is difficult to arouse collective concern for challenging racism or any form of domination. The will to resist can be tamed by a world that says everything can be as you want in the world of fantasy. And consumer culture generates the fantasy.

When it comes to race, the ads tell us there is no racism, that "we are the world." Racially diverse ads evoke a shared culture of consumerism where there is no racial divide; oneness is attained by mutual consumption. Martin Luther King's vision of a beloved community gets translated into a multicultural multiethnic shopping spree. Commitment to consumption above all else unifies diverse races and classes. Everyone is a cannibal feasting on everything and everyone. In a *New York Times* magazine segment focusing on selfishness, a twenty-one-year-old student is quoted in Andrew Cherlin's article "I'm O.K., You're Selfish" declaring: "I just think it's a 'me-me' world. Everything is focused on what you can accomplish, what you can do and how far you can go." And the success of these accomplishments, of these journeys is always measured by how much you can buy.

While we live in a culture where racism prevails, where the limited gains in civil rights for people of color and all women are daily assaulted, a society where racial and class apartheid is a norm, the world of spending is the one place where the promise of community is evoked. No matter your class, no matter your race, if you have access to credit, to cash, every store is open to you. In the world of spending, desire for the commodity matters, it cuts across all barriers. In this world there is no need of social awareness, for radical protest. And that world is particularly appealing to a generation of youth who are caught up in the fantasy world that advertising produces, a world where everyone is one, where there is no pain, and everyone can belong if they can pay the price of the ticket.

In reality lots of young people cannot pay the price of the ticket. The downside of fantasies of a classless society, of a consumer-driven dream wherein you are what you possess, is the psychological torment it causes everyone who is unable to fulfill endless material longings. A dimension of that psychological torment is envy. Among young people, from grade school age kids to teenagers, to lack signs of material success is to be marked as worthless and to be the object of shame. That shame may be externalized and internalized. It converges with envy. In John Bradshaw's *Healing the Shame that Binds You,* he contends: "The most childish form of envy is greed. . . . The envier magically believes that if he possesses that quality, he would be okay. Envy in the form of greed is exploited by modern advertising, which offers the posthypnotic suggestion that we are what we possess." Among the poor this envy-based greed has produced a predatory culture where young people randomly slaughter each other over material possessions. And this same murderous longing manifests among youth who are not materially deprived but whose material longings are grandiose. Confronted with young peers who have greater degrees of privilege they also slander and slaughter.

In recent years popular movies directed at teens, like the film *Clueless,* which became a television series, poke fun at the ridiculous values of the wealthy world even as they glamorize possessions. In *Clueless,* much of the movie's plot centers around the accumulation and admiration of possessions. In this movie, the star of the show is rich, white, blonde, blue eyed, and thin to the point of being anorexic. She has as her faithful sidekick a less materially privileged black friend who constantly expresses admiration and envy. In the popular imagination the longing to be rich is depicted as not just a positive aspiration, but the only aspiration that has meaning. The most recent version of this theme is the movie *Anywhere But Here,* where the teenage heroine is encouraged by a middle-aged divorced mom to lie, cheat, steal, do anything she can to be chosen by the rich, and live as they do. When the film begins, the daughter is hypercritical of her mother's obsessive insistence that you are what you possess, but as the film progresses she colludes with her. Presented as light entertainment, watched by youth of all ages, these films deny class conflict. Yet grade schools and high schools are the places where class conflict is bitterly expressed through the constant shaming of kids who lack material privilege.

On an episode of the television show *South Park,* one of the students asks the teacher why it is that poor people always smell like sour milk. She does not challenge this perception. Instead, she tacitly acknowledges that it is a perception she shares, by simply saying that she does not know why this is the case. Many schools in our nation have insisted that pupils wear uniforms to intervene on the wide-spread violence that was taking place in relation to material posses-sions. One way poor tough kids wage war against materially privi-leged kids is to forcefully take their stuff. Lots of middle-class kids leave public schools, where the educational standards are excellent, to avoid conflict over material possessions.

Ironically, our nation is full of young people, especially teenagers, who deny the reality of class, even as they identify solely with the values and mores of a predatory ruling class. Children from poor backgrounds are isolated and self-isolated because being poor is always and only a cause of shame. And while that has to some extent been the case throughout our nation's history, it was much easier for poor youth to mask class backgrounds with clothing and education. But when the notion that you are what you possess becomes the norm, and the possessions are no longer defined as simply decent goods but rather extremely costly luxury items, then the gap between those who have nothing much, those who have a little, and those who have a lot widens. Children raised in working-class and poor homes in the late fifties and sixties grew up in an environment where the clothing of the working class constituted what was chic, sym-bolized by blue jeans, overalls, or the peasant skirts made from bed-spreads. This clothing was all part of a critique of class power. First popular in countercultures, it became an expression of class defiance by the children of the rich and well-off. It fostered the belief that class could be transcended. And more importantly, that privileged-class groups might be enriched by associating with the working class and/or poor.

Those are yesterday's visions. Today's youth who are among the thirty-eight million or more poor citizens of this society or who are members of working-class groups want to leave their class origins behind. Like their peers from privileged groups they do not think about a range of class positionalities. To them one is either rich or poor and there is no in-between, nothing else matters.

In part, youth culture's worship of wealth stems from the fact that it is easier to acquire money and goods than it is to find meaningful values and ethics, to know who you are and what you want to become, to make and sustain and friends, to know love. The pursuit of wealth may breed greed and envy but it may also breed ambition. And while the young are fueled with the ambition to get ahead, to make as much money as possible, all attention can be deflected away from emotional lack. When materially privileged white high school boys slaughter students who are different from them, from different races and classes, it is easier for the nation to talk about the luxury cars they drove rather than to talk about the emotional emptiness and nihilism that permeate their psyches. If their worship of death is linked solely to too much luxury, to many material possessions, then the fantasy that cutting back on these items will remedy what ails them and their peers can prevail.

Often parents of all classes who are themselves critical of the worship of money, of ruling class groups, still feel compelled to teach their children that money is the most important thing in life. Materially privileged parents who may themselves eschew luxuries often encourage materialistic hedonism in their children. Among poor youth, lust for luxury made synonymous with personal worth and value has supported predatory drug cultures, which bring huge sums of money into their lives. The artifacts that money buys are the sign that one is important, that one has power. Adults who once held different values are persuaded by young people that money is all that is important. This struggle between the ethical values of an older black generation and a young generation eager to get rich quick was a central theme in Lorraine Hansberry's powerful play *A Raisin in the Sun*. The child of parents who have worked hard to provide their children with a good life, Walter Lee wants to take the insurance money the family receives when his father dies and use it to buy a liquor store. His mother sees the money as providing them with the opportunity to challenge racial discrimination in housing, to live in a better neighborhood. In her ethical universe, money is only useful when it enhances one's overall well-being. In Walter Lee's universe, having money is the sole determinant of one's well-being. At a key moment in the drama, his mother expresses her outrage at his values asking him "since when did money become life." He responds by telling her, "It was always life, mama. We just did not know it."

No study has been done to document the extent to which children living with divorced mothers with low incomes find these relationships changed when kids choose to live with fathers who have better incomes and can buy more. In some cases the children may know that their emotional growth is better fostered with their mothers, but they want to be where the money is because that it is what they are told will determine their value and, ultimately, their lot in life. They are told this by mass media, by the culture of greed surrounding them. Single mothers who struggle with impoverishment, who work to make ends meet, often send a double message because circumstances compel them to focus centrally and occasionally obsessively on material matters even as they may be trying to teach their children a set of values where material needs and desires do not matter more than bonds of love and care, etc.

Sociologists have yet to link the extreme materialism of today's youth with the economic changes that enter their lives through divorce or the failure of fathers to financially contribute. In part, their obsession with material goods stems from a deep-seated fear that they will possibly suffer ongoing material deprivation. Those fears have a reality base. And unless they are appropriately addressed they can lead to intense preoccupation with material consumption. Of course, this is equally true for children who suffer ongoing material lack. The difference lies in the fact that poor children who have never known material well-being rarely feel either a sense of entitlement, that is, that something that should rightly be theirs without effort has been denied them, or the despair that the material privilege they once had is no longer a part of their reality. Usually kids from impoverished backgrounds have a more realistic awareness of class even though this does not ensure that they will be protected from the brainwashing of a larger culture, which encourages us all to see our self-worth as linked always and only to material wealth.

The institutionalized church or temple, which once played a major role in creating both a compassionate image of the poor as well as compassionate identification with the poor, has no meaningful impact on the worldview of today's young no matter their class or race. While young black gangsta' rappers stand up at award ceremonies and give thanks to God for their fame and fortune, the Christian or Islamic religous beliefs they evoke do not shape their moral values or their actions in the world. They (and their nonblack counterparts) mock their gods, and their wanton worship of wealth encourages the young to believe that God is useful only as a tool for taking you to the top. And this top is not Martin Luther King's mountaintop where he felt given a divine vision of social justice and democratic union.

This is the generation of the young who worship at the throne of the assassins who mock, ridicule, and destroy every value or ethical belief that challenges the rule of the dollar. This generation has blood on its hands and does not care as long as the blood can be washed away by fancy soaps, aromatherapy, and a host of other little luxuries. When the politics of greed rule, the young are particularly vulnerable. Without a core identity, belief system, or place within a beloved community, they lack the resources to ward off the awesome allure that says unprecedented wealth awaits everyone, that we have only to imagine. When the deluded young are forced to face the reality that we are bound by class, by limited resources, by the exhaustion of glories, by endless exploitation, they become rage filled and rage addicted. Only death, self-mutilation, or the slaughter of their peers appeases. They cannot kill the oppressor because they do not know who the oppressor is. They do not understand class politics or capitalism. In their minds, to be without money is to be without life.

Without education for critical consciousness that begins when children are entering the world of consumer capitalism, there will never be a set of basic values that can ward off the politics of predatory greed. Seeds of hope are planted in the efforts made by youth to shift from focusing on luxury items and designer clothes to a grunge, back-to-nature lifestyle, by the radicalized young who work for environmental rights, and by the young who are facing the realities of class and working to create a just society.

8

Class and Race: The New Black Elite

Collectively, black folks in the United States have never wanted to highlight the issue of class and class exploitation, even though there have always been diverse caste and class groups among African-Americans. Racist biases shaped historical scholarship so that the information about African explorers who came to the Americas before Columbus was suppressed along with elementary knowledge of the black folks who came as explorers and immigrants who were never slaves. Indeed, until recently most black people telling the story of our presence here in the so-called New World would begin that narrative with slavery. They would not talk about the Africans who came here bringing gifts of cotton seed, or the small numbers of black immigrants who came seeking the same freedom as their white counterparts.

While a few white Americans are willing to acknowledge that a large majority of the European colonizers who came to these shores were indigents and working-class folks seeking to improve their lot, mostly they tell the story of their arrival on these shores by calling attention to the journeys of the privileged. Like their black counterparts, those whites who could count themselves among the privileged were few. The vast majority of whites who entered states of indentured servitude were working class and poor. Yet the journeys of the privileged have come to constitute the norm "white" colonizer and/or immigrant experience, whereas the norm for black people continues to be slavery.

Annals of history do let us know that there was caste and class division between the small number of free blacks and the majority of the enslaved black population. More often than not racial solidarity forged a bond between black-skinned folks even if they did not share the same caste or class standing. They were bonded by the knowledge that at any moment, whether free or enslaved, they could share the same fate.

This did not mean that free blacks did not at times "lord" it over their enslaved counterparts. Nor did enslavement keep some black folks from emulating white colonizers by embracing a color caste hierarchy wherein fair-skinned individuals had higher rank than their white counterparts. This hierarchy based on color would later be reflected in postslavery class divisions. Since racially mixed slaves often received greater material benefits from their slaveholding white relatives even when those relatives did not publicly acknowledge these blood ties, they often had more resources than their darker counterparts.

Despite segregation and legal racial apartheid, by the onset of the twentieth century distinct class divisions were emerging in segregated black communities. Still, racial solidarity became even more the norm as postslavery white exploitation and oppression intensified. The logic of racial uplift meant that black folks on the bottom of the class hierarchy were encouraged to regard with admiration and respect peers who were gaining class power. In those days, the tiny privileged black middle class was not seen as the enemy of the working poor and indigent. They were examples that it was possible for everyone to rise. It was this belief that informed W. E. B. DuBois' vision of a talented tenth that would lead efforts to uplift the race and change the collective lot of African-Americans. In 1903 he emphasized this point, insisting that it was important to develop "the Best of this race that they may guide the Mass away from the contamination and death of the Worst, in their own and other races." By 1948 he critiqued this earlier supposition stating: "When I came out of college into the world of work, I realized that it was quite possible that my plan of training a talented tenth might put in control and power, a group of selfish, self-indulgent, well-to-do men, whose basic interest in solving the Negro Problem was personal; personal freedom and unhampered enjoyment and use of the world, without any real care, or certainly no arousing care, as to what became of the mass of American Negroes, or of the mass of any people." Growing up in the fifties, I was acutely aware of the contempt black folks with class privilege directed toward the masses.

In our segregated town, the black folks with relative class power, whom group sociologist E. Franklin Frazier would later identify as the black bourgeoisie, enjoyed their role as mediators between the black masses and the white folks who were really in charge. They openly espoused contempt for less-privileged black folks even as they needed that group to stay on the bottom so they could measure how far up they had gotten by how far down the black masses remained. At the end of the day, no matter our class, all black folks lived together in segregated neighborhoods. The surrounding white supremacist world reminded all of us through exploitation and domination that even the richest black person could be crushed by racism's heavy weight.

That sense of solidarity was altered by a class-based civil rights struggle whose ultimate goal was to acquire more freedom for those black folks who already had a degree of class privilege however relative. By the late 1960s class-based racial integration disrupted the racial solidarity that often held black folks together despite class difference. Pressured to assimilate into mainstream white culture to increase their class power and status, privileged black individuals began to leave the underprivileged behind, moving into predominately white neighborhoods, taking their money and their industry out of the segregated black world. Historically, white colleges and universities had not yet hired the best and the brightest of black thinkers. Anti-racist sentiment was not the reason for racial integration. Strategically, white politicians recognized the threat that a decolonized militant self-determined black population could pose to the existing status quo.

Desegregation was the way to weaken the collective radicalization of black people that had been generated by militant civil rights and black power movement. It was better to give privileged black people greater access to the existing social structure than to have a radical talented tenth that would lead the black masses to revolt and cultural revolution. Concurrently, a shift in global politics had made it apparent that white people would have to do business with people of color globally to maintain U.S. imperialist economic domination. The old colonialism could not form the basis of contemporary economic exchanges globally. It was vital that new generations of white people learn to relate in new and different ways to people of color globally if the ruling class power of the United States was to remain intact. Given these concerns racial integration was useful. It diffused politics of racial uplift and black radicalization and simultaneously produced a new class of privileged upwardly mobile black folks who would see their interests as more allied with the existing white power structure than with any group of black people. After years of collective struggle, by the end of the sixties liberal individualism had become more the norm for black folks, particularly the black bourgeoisie, more so than the previous politics of communalism, which emphasized racial uplift and sharing resources.

In the community of my growing up it was not difficult to distinguish those black folks with class privilege who were committed to racial uplift, to sharing resources, and those who were eager to exploit the community solely for their own individual gain. The latter were fixated on making money, on flaunting their status and power. They were not respected or revered. That, however, began to change as market values wiped out core beliefs in the integrity of communalism and shared resources, replacing them with the edict that every woman and man "live for yoself, for yoself and nobody else."

Traditional black communities, like the one I grew up in, which had always included everyone, all classes, were changed by the end of the seventies. Folks with money took their money out of the community. Local black-owned business all but ceased with the exception of the undertakers. Exercising their equal rights as citizens, black folks began to live, and most importantly, to shop, everywhere, seemingly not noticing the changes in predominately black communities. These changes happened all over the United States. By the early nineties, the black poor and underclass were fast becoming isolated segregated communities. Big business, in the form of a booming drug trade, infiltrated these communities and let addiction and the violence it breeds and sustains chip away and ultimately erode the overall well-being of the poor, and working-class black folks left.

Militant black power advocates of the sixties (many of whom were from privileged class backgrounds) successfully working to end racism, to feed the poor, and raise the consciousness of all would no doubt be shocked to see gates walling off indigent black communities all around this nation. The black middle and upper class in no way protest these modern-day concentration camps. Historical amnesia sets in and they conveniently forget that the fascists who engineered the Nazi holocaust did not begin with gas chambers but rather began their genocidal agenda by hoarding people together and depriving them of the basic necessities of life—adequate food, shelter, health care, etc. Lethal drugs like crack cocaine make gas chambers unnecessary in these modern times. Without outright naming, concentration camp–like conditions now exist in this nation in all major urban communities. Like their uncaring counterparts in other racial groups, most black privileged folks need never enter these communities, need never see the slow genocide that takes place there. They can choose to stand at a distance and blame the victims.

A thriving, corrupt "talented tenth" have not only emerged as the power brokers preaching individual liberalism and black capitalism to everyone (especially the black masses), their biggest commodity is "selling blackness." They make sure they mask their agenda so black capitalism looks like black self-determination. Whether it is movies made by black filmmakers that glamorize and celebrate black on black predatory violence while placing blame on the victims, or literature produced by black academics and/or writers that does the same, it is evident that the vast majority of privileged class black folks feel they have nothing in common with the black poor. Whenever well-to-do black persons justly complain about the ways racism operates to keep them from reaching the highest pinnacle of career success or the way everyday racism makes it hard for them to get a taxi or does not exempt them from being treated unjustly by the police, if these complaints are not linked to an acknowledgment of how their class power mediates racial injustice in a way that it does not for the poor and underprivileged, they collude in the nation's refusal to acknowledge the solace and protection class privilege affords them.

Prior to civil rights and militant black power struggle, class privilege did little to help upwardly mobile black folks if white folks wanted to exploit and oppress them with impunity. This is no longer the case. This does not mean that racism does not daily assault black people with class privilege; it does. The pain of the privileged is linked to the pain of the indigent who also daily suffer racial assault, just as anti-racist struggle to end that suffering promises liberation to all classes. However, as the gap between privileged blacks and the black poor widens, all who are truly committed to justice and an end to racial domination must break through the denial that allows the haves to disavow the myriad ways class privilege mediates the pain of racial assault. The black working class, poor, and underclass cannot use class status and privilege to escape racial assault or to pacify wounds when they are inflicted.

In large and small ways middle-class, upper-class, and wealthy black people can create lifestyles that enable them to minimize contact with harsh racism. Numerous privileged black folks hire white underlings to interface between them and a racist white world. Assimilation is yet another strategy they deploy to deflect harsh racism away from them and onto "other" blacks. Ellis Closs's book *The Rage of the Black Middle Class* reminded everyone that class privilege does not mean that well-off blacks will not suffer racial assault, and it enrages them. Yet he did not link their rage with a rage against the conditions imposed upon the black poor and indigent by white supremacist exploitation and oppression. While all our rage at racism is justifiable, it undermines anti-racist struggle and the call for social justice when well-off black folks attempt to create a social context where they will be exempt from racist assault even as the underprivileged remain daily victimized.

Nowadays, practically every public representation of blackness is created by black folks who are materially privileged. More often than not they speak about the black poor and working class but not with them, or on their behalf. The presence of a small number of privileged black folks who continue to work for justice, who work to change this culture so that all black people can live fully and well, is often obscured by the dominant white culture's focus on those who are fundamentally opportunistic and/or corrupt. These conservative black elites, chosen and appointed to positions of authority by the mainstream, not only take charge of interrupting and shaping public policy that will affect the lives of underprivileged black folks, they police black folks who do not agree with them or support their agendas. That policing may take the form of preventing folks from getting jobs, getting heard if they speak and/or write publicly, or deploying various forms of psychological terrorism.

When possible they use their class power to censor and silence, deploying their greater access to white mainstream media, and all other avenues of power, in ways that discredit dissenting black voices. They censor and isolate these voices to diffuse the power of those lone individuals who care for justice enough to link word and deed, theory and practice. Ideologically, they perpetuate the false assumption that everyone is really corrupt, that all privileged class blacks by virtue of their achievements and status betray those without privilege. As this thinking gains widespread acceptance they need not worry about critique or exposure. They take advantage of the fact that the poor and underclass masses know nothing about their lives and have no power to expose their contradictions or their betrayals. They isolate and ignore dissenting voices whether they come from progressive visionary underprivileged sources or their more radical privileged class counterparts.

More individual black folks than ever before are entering the ranks of the rich and upper class. Allegiance to their class interests usually supersedes racial solidarity. They are not only leaving the underprivileged black masses behind, they collude in the systems of domination that ensure the continued exploitation and oppression of the poor. Unlike many of their middle-class peers who may be bonded with lower-class and poor people, who are compelled by kinship ties to share resources, they refuse identification with the black poor, unless it serves their interests to act concerned. Michael Jordan, one of the richest men in the world, epitomizes this perspective. His commitment to capitalist profit at any cost has characterized his economic success. For mainstream culture he is the global example that colonized mind can strengthen one's class power. There are many wealthy and upper-class black people who "think like Mike" but they are not in the public eye, or if they are visible they do not openly reveal their identification with the values of a ruling class elite.

When Harvard academic Henry Louis Gates, Jr., deemed by mainstream white culture to be one of the most powerful black spokespersons in this society, did a program for public television where he candidly challenged the notion that black people across class share common perspectives, he was subject to forms of critique that had not previously characterized black folks' response to his success. Even so, he and many folks like him live in and conduct business in a world where black people's response, whether positive or negative, is not perceived as influential or important. Black people do not have the power to invite the black elite to the White House and do not reward them with unprecedented fame, status, and financial remuneration.

The miseducation of all underprivileged black groups strengthens the class power of the nonprogressive black elite. Without anti-racist reparations, a central one being affirmative action programs, which once offered financial aid to the poor and working class, these groups are not allowed entry into the ranks of the talented tenth. Since they are the individuals who are best situated to experientially understand the dynamics of class among black folks, who may retain allegiance to their class of origins and breed dissent in the world of the privileged, denying them access to higher education is a strategic act of repression. Without quality education, which broadens the mind and strengthens one's capacity to think critically, they are less likely to threaten the status quo. Increasingly, there are few black folks from poor and working-class backgrounds being educated in elite settings. They simply do not have the means. Those select few who receive aid are far more likely to share the conservative perspectives of their well-to-do counterparts.

Unlike my generation (poor and working-class children of the late sixties and seventies), who were able to receive college educations because of financial aid but were not seduced by the fantasy of becoming rich or entering the ranks of the mainstream black elite, as that elite was not yet in place, the underprivileged today are more tempted by the goodies offered by the status quo. Since they have no organized visionary radical movement for social justice to make them more conscious and to sustain them should they rebel, they fear dissent. They are more likely than not to claim that racism has ended or that if it exists it does not affect them. They are more likely to believe

that the economic plight of the black masses is caused by a lack of
skills, will, and know-how and not by systemic exploitation and
oppression. They have learned to think this way from the lessons
mainstream culture teaches them about what they must do to succeed. They stand ready to ascend to the heights of class privilege by
any means necessary. And now more than ever there is a corrupt talented tenth in place to guide them along the way.

Significantly, even though a growing majority of privileged-class
black folks condemn and betray the black poor and underclass, they
avoid critique and confrontation themselves by not focusing on their
class power. In the nineties they prefer to talk about race and ignore
class. All black people know that no matter your class you will suffer
wounds inflicted by racism, however relative. Fewer black people
know intimately the concrete everyday ways class power and privilege mediate this pain, allowing some black folks to live luxuriously
despite racism. Sadly, to escape this pain or to shield themselves from
the genocide that is assaulting black masses, they surrender all trans-
formative forms of racial solidarity in anti-racist struggle to protect
their class interests. They betray their people even as they maintain
their status and public image by pretending that they know best and
are best positioned to protect the collective public good of all black
people irrespective of class.

The black masses are encouraged by an empowered privileged
few to believe that any critique they or anyone makes of the class
power of black elites is merely sour grapes. Or they are made to feel
they are interfering with racial uplift and racial solidarity if they want
to talk about class. They live the reality of class divisions among black
people. Unlike the black elite, they are not ashamed or afraid to talk
about class; they simply have little or no public venues in which to air
their views. Radical black voices, especially those with some degree
of class privilege, must have the courage to talk about class. Racial
solidarity in anti-racist struggle can, sometimes does, and must coexist
with a recognition of the importance of ending class elitism.

Vigilant critique of the politics of class in diverse black communities is and should be a dynamic dimension of all progressive struggles for black self-determination. Being upwardly mobile need not mean that one betrays the people on the bottom. Yet we need to know more about the concrete ways we can have a degree of class privilege without abandoning allegiance to those who are underprivileged or accountability for their fate. Progressive black folks who have class privilege must intervene when our more conservative and liberal counterparts seek to deny the reality of black on black class cruelty and exploitation.

We must courageously challenge the privileged who aggressively seek to deny the disadvantaged a chance to change their lot. Privileged people are the individuals who create representations of blackness where education is deemed valueless, where violence is glamorous, where the poor are dehumanized. These images are not just produced by white folks. Understanding that many black people seeking success in the existing white supremacist capitalist patriarchy embrace white supremacist thought and action, we need sophisticated strategies to challenge and resist their exploitation and oppression of the masses. Saying that they are not "black" or that they are "Uncle Toms" is a shallow critique that does not address in any meaningful way the reality that any viable anti-racist movement for social justice must have a program aimed at decolonizing and converting those black folks who act in collusion with the status quo. Conversion empowers; judgmental assaults alienate.

Until visionary black thinkers, from all walks of life, can create strategies and lifestyles that embrace the idea of empowerment without domination for all classes, all efforts toward black self-determination will fail. Were the black poor and underclass able to create constructive class solidarity, there would be hope that their needs would be articulated and addressed. Progressive black "elites" must humanely confront and challenge conservative peers. It is our task to forge a vision of solidarity in ending domination, which includes anti-racist struggle that realistically confronts class difference and constructively intervenes on the growing class antagonism between black folks with class privilege and the black masses who are daily being stripped of class power. While we need not return to the notion of leadership by a talented tenth, we do need to draw on the legacy of constant radical commitment to social justice for all, which undergirds the dream of liberatory black self-determination that was at the heart of DuBois' vision.

9

Feminism and Class Power

Revolutionary feminist thinking has always raised the issue of classism among women. From the onset, there has been a struggle within feminist movement between the reformist model of liberation, which basically demands equal rights for women within the existing class struggle, and more radical and/or revolutionary models, which call for fundamental change in the existing structure so that models of mutuality and equality can replace old paradigms. Just as militant black liberation struggle calling for an end to classism was made to appear unnecessary, once black folks gained greater access to jobs, revolutionary feminism was dismissed by mainstream reformist feminism when women, primarily well-educated white women with class privilege, began to achieve equal access to class power with their male counterparts.

When contemporary feminist movement first began, it received mass media attention solely because of the presence of privileged class women rebelling against their class and patriarchal hierarchy within that class. As a consequence, the issues that received public attention were not those most relevant to working women or masses of women. A small group of elite privileged class white women were the group Betty Friedan wrote about when she identified "the problem that has no name," a phrase used to euphemistically describe the dissatisfaction individuals felt about being confined and subordinated in the home as housewives. Their issue was informed by both the politics of gender and class because while they were complaining about the dangers of confinement in the home, a huge majority of women in the nation were in the workforce. And many of these working women, who put in long hours for low wages while still doing all the work in the domestic household, would have seen the right to stay home as "freedom."

It was not gender discrimination or sexist oppression that had kept privileged women from working outside the home; it was the fact that the work open to them would have been the same low-paid unskilled labor open to all working women. This elite group of highly educated females stayed at home rather than do the type of work large numbers of middle-income and working-class women were doing. Occasionally, a few of these women wanted to work outside the home and did so, performing tasks way below their educational skills, oftentimes facing resistance from their husbands. It was this resistance that turned the issue of their working outside the home into an issue of gender discrimination and made opposing patriarchy the political platform for change rather than class struggle.

From the onset, reformist white women with class privilege were well aware that the power and freedom they wanted was the freedom they perceived men of their class enjoying. Their resistance to patriarchal male domination in the domestic household provided them with a connection they could use to unite across class with other women who were weary of male domination. Women who were lesbians, of all races and classes, were at the forefront of the radicalization of contemporary female resistance to patriarchy in part because this group had by their sexual preference already placed themselves outside the domain of heterosexist privilege and protection, both in the home and in the workplace. No matter their class, they were social outcasts, the objects of patriarchal abuse and scorn. Concurrently, unlike their heterosexual counterparts, they were not relying on men to support them economically. They needed and wanted equal pay for equal work. Much revolutionary and/or radical feminist thought was produced by lesbians who had a longer personal history of challenging patriarchal conceptions of women's roles.

Lesbian feminist theorists were among the first to raise the issue of class in collective and consciousness-raising groups expressing their viewpoints in an accessible language. Well-educated leftist straight women writing about class often remained trapped in academic jargon that kept them from sharing their message with the female masses. In the early seventies, anthologies like *Class and Feminism,* edited by Charlotte Bunch and Nancy Myron, published essays written by women from diverse class backgrounds who were confronting the issue of classism in their feminist collective. Each essay emphasized the fact that class was not simply a question of money. In "The Last Straw," Rita Mae Brown (who was not a famous writer at the time) clearly stated: "Class is much more than Marx's definition of relationship to the means of production. Class involves your behavior, your basic assumptions, how you are taught to behave, what you expect from yourself and from others, your concept of a future, how you understand problems and solve them, how you think, feel, act." Those women who entered feminist groups made up of diverse classes were the first to see that the vision of a united sisterhood where all females joined to fight patriarchy could not emerge until the issue of class was confronted.

Of course once class was placed on the agenda, women had to face the intersections of class and race. And when they did, it was evident that black women were clearly at the bottom of this society's economic totem pole. Initially, well-educated white women from working-class backgrounds were more visible than black females of all classes in feminist movement. They were a minority within the movement but they were the voice of experience. They knew better than their privileged-class white sisters the costs of resisting race, class, and gender domination. They knew what it was like to move from the bottom up. Between them and their privileged-class comrades there was a conflict over appropriate behavior. Describing how these different class experiences were expressed in their essay "Revolution Begins at Home," Coletta Reid and Charlotte Bunch stated: "Often, middle and especially upper middle class women for whom things have come easily develop a privileged passivity. Someone with privilege can conveniently think that it's not necessary to fight or discipline herself to get anything. Everything will work out. Because she has made it by following nice middle class rules of life, she doesn't like for people to be pushy, dogmatic, hostile or intolerant." Within radical feminist movement, women from privileged-class backgrounds learned the concrete politics of class struggle confronting challenges made by less-privileged women but also learning from them assertiveness skills and constructive ways to cope with conflict.

In reformist circles, however, privileged white women often made it clear to the women who did not share their class status and/or color that this was their movement, that they were in charge, and their needs would determine the agenda. Reformist feminist issues centered on gaining social equality with privileged men within the existing social structure. These concerns neatly coincided with white supremacist capitalist patriarchal fears that white power would diminish if nonwhite people gained equal access to economic power and privilege. Supporting what in effect became white power reformist feminism enabled the mainstream white male patriarchy to bolster its power while simultaneously undermining the radical politics of feminism. Revolutionary white feminist thinkers expressed outrage at co-optation in the alternative press. In her collection of essays *The Coming of Black Genocide,* Mary Barfoot boldy states:"There are white women, hurt and angry, who believed that the seventies women's movement meant sisterhood, and who feel betrayed by escalator women. By women who went back home to the patriarchy. But the women's movement never left the father Dick's side. . . . There was no war. And there was no liberation. We got a share of genocide profits and we love it. We are Sisters of Patriarchy, and true supporters of national and class oppression. . . . Patriarchy in its highest form is Euro-imperialism on a world scale. If we're Dick's sister and want what he has gotten, then in the end we support that system that he got it all from." Reformist white women were not alone in their betrayal of more radical feminist concerns.

Many upwardly mobile women of color who had ambivalent attitudes toward feminism jumped on the bandwagon to reap benefits (job promotion, status as leaders, etc.) garnered by struggles for gender justice. Like their white peers they used feminism to enhance their class status and power. The class-based academization of American feminism created the context for its deradicalization and for the takeover of gender studies by opportunistic women and men who were simply not interested in radically changing society. Ironically, focus on race and racism was one of the new directions in feminist thought that deflected attention away from issues of class. While many feminist white women slowly became more willing to talk about race and confess racism in the eighties, they did not speak about their classism, their fear, condescension, and outright hatred of the poor and working class. By the nineties, white women had managed to incorporate race comfortably into existing gender studies without linking this academic work to any organized feminist movement challenging white supremacist capitalist patriarchy.

As privileged women gained greater access to economic power with privileged class men, feminist discussions of class were no longer commonplace. Instead, women were encouraged to see the economic gains of affluent females as a positive sign for all women. In actuality, these gains rarely changed the lot of poor and working-class women. And since privileged class men did not become caretakers in the domestic household, the freedom of privileged class women of all races required the sustained subordination of working-class women. When privileged women left the home to work, someone had to stay in the home and do the dirty work.

There was simply no way for women with class privilege who wanted to garner economic power and status while simultaneously holding on to their feminist credentials to confront the issue of class. Since patriarchal men of all classes had not joined feminist revolution and changed their consciousness and behavior in order for privileged-class women, most of them white, to fully reap the benefits of equal access to men of their class, they had to accept and condone continued economic exploitation and subordination on the basis of gender for working-class and poor women. For example: It had not been politically correct, when feminist movement began, to exploit another woman—more often than not an immigrant woman of color (paying low wages, unreasonable working hours)—to tend your children and clean your house so that you might become "liberated" and work outside the home. As the movement progressed and women gained greater class power, these practices became acceptable.

In the nineties, collusion with the existing social structure was the price of so-called liberation. At the end of the day, most privileged class white women and their upwardly mobile peers of other races wanted class privilege and social equality with men of their class more than freedom for themselves and their exploited and oppressed sisters. This collusion helped destabilize feminist movement. It substantiated the critique of reformist feminism, which argued that white men supported equal rights for women in the workplace as a way of bolstering the waning class power of upper- and middle-class white families (which was the direct consequence of economic depression). Concurrently, it directly undermined affirmative action gains made by civil rights struggle on behalf of black people as white women quickly became the primary beneficiaries.

When women acquired greater class status and class power without conducting themselves in ways different from males, feminist politics were undermined. Lots of women felt betrayed. Middle- and lower-middle-class women who were suddenly compelled by the ethos of feminism to enter the workforce did not feel "liberated" once they faced the hard truth that working outside the home did not mean work in the home would be shared. No-fault divorce proved to be more economically beneficial to men than women. Spouses in longtime marriages who had been supported economically by privileged and or working-class husbands while they worked without wages inside the home suffered economically as divorce became more common. These women felt betrayed both by the conventional sexism, which had sanctioned their stay-at-home housewife role, and by the feminism, which insisted work was liberating without making it clear that there would be few job opportunities available to older women of any class who had spent most of their adult lives unemployed.

As many black women and other women of color saw white women from privileged classes benefiting economically more than any other group from reformist feminist gains in the workforce, it simply reaffirmed that feminism was a white woman thing. To the men of those groups, it gave added credence to their insistence that women's lib had been from the onset a way to keep the working black man/man of color in his place. These sexist men were not interested in joining with radical and/or revolutionary feminist thinkers to overthrow reformist feminist control of the movement and put in place more progressive strategies.

Radical and/or revolutionary feminism has continued to put forth a vision of feminist movement that critiques and challenges classism. Unlike shallow reformist feminist insistence that work is liberatory, the visionary paradigm for social change insists that education for critical consciousness is the first step in the process of feminist transformation. Hence women, men, and children can be advocates of feminist politics whether they work or not. Then intervention within all arenas of the existing structures is the next step. That intervention may take the form of reform or radical change. For example: Radical and/or revolutionary feminists who created feminist theory but lacked doctorates recognized that our work would be completely ignored if we did not enter more fully into the existing patriarchal academic system. For some of us, that meant working to get Ph.D.'s even though we were not that interested in academic careers. To succeed within that system we had to develop strategies enabling us to do our work without compromising our feminist politics and values. This was not an easy task, yet we accomplished it. Some of us from working-class backgrounds changed our class status and entered the ranks of class privilege. We understood economic self-sufficiency to be a crucial goal of feminist movement. However, we also believed, a belief now affirmed by experience, that it was possible for us to gain class power without betraying our solidarity toward those without class privilege. One way that we achieved this end was by living simply, sharing our resources, and refusing to engage in hedonistic consumerism and the politics of greed. Our goals were not to become wealthy but to become economically self-sufficient. Our experiences counter the assumption that women could only gain economically by colluding with the existing capitalist patriarchy.

Unfortunately, the work of radical and/or revolutionary feminist thinkers, female and male, rarely receives widespread attention. When it does, it is often discredited by conservative factions posing as feminists. A basic definition of feminism is that it is a movement to end sexism and sexist exploitation and oppression. One cannot be feminist and conservative; it is a fundamental contradiction. Of course, conservative and liberal pro-patriarchy women protecting their class interests have effectively used mass media to blur the issues and make it seem that feminism can be all things to all people. Since reformist feminist thinkers who make it into the mainstream have a stake in obscuring radical theory and practice, they collude with the forces of conservative patriarchy to make it appear feminist movement no longer matters, that we are in a "postfeminist" stage and that freedom is an impossibility. This position makes gaining goodies within the existing class structure the only hope. Ironically, anti-feminist public policy is steadily undermining the rights gained by feminist struggle so women who have gained class privilege by colluding with white supremacist capitalist patriarchy will lose in the long run.

The only genuine hope of feminist liberation lies with a vision of social change that takes into consideration the ways interlocking systems of classism, racism, and sexism work to keep women exploited and oppressed. Western women have gained class power and greater gender inequality because a global white supremacist patriarchy enslaves and/or subordinates masses of Third World women. In this country the combined forces of a booming prison industry and workfare-oriented welfare in conjunction with conservative immigration politics create the conditions for indentured slavery to be condoned. Ending welfare will create a new underclass of women and children to be abused and exploited by the existing structures of domination, making it more evident that the "freedom" of women with class privilege depends on the enslavement of subordinated groups.

Given the changing realities of class in our nation, widening gaps between the rich and poor, the continued feminization of poverty, we desperately need a mass-based radical feminist movement that can build on the strength of the past, including the positive gains generated by reform, while showing new direction and offering meaningful interrogation of existing feminist thinking and action that was simply wrongminded. Significantly, a visionary movement would root its work first and foremost in the concrete conditions of working-class and poor women. That means creating a movement wherein education for critical consciousness begins where people are. There is still time for us to put in place low-income housing that women can own. Were working-class and poor women given the opportunity to own their housing through progressive workfare/welfare, this would be a step toward freedom. The creation of housing co-ops with feminist principles is another step that could make feminist struggle relevant to the masses. These are just a few examples of work that needs to be done.

Despite the ways reformist thinkers manipulated class issues to undermine feminist politics, it remains the only movement for social justice in our society that focuses in a primary way on the concerns of women and children. If women are to play a meaningful role in struggles to end racism and classism, they need to begin with feminist consciousness. To abandon feminist movement is another gesture of collusion. Radical/revolutionary feminist politics bring a message of hope as well as strategies to empower women and men of all classes. Feminism is for everybody.

10

White Poverty: The Politics of Invisibility

In the southern world of racial apartheid I grew up in, no racialized class division was as intense or as fraught with bitter conflict as the one between poor whites and black folks. All black people knew that white skin gave any southern "cracker or peckerwood" (ethnic slurs reserved for the white poor) more power and privilege than even the wealthiest of black folks. However, these slurs were not the product of black vernacular slang, they were the terms white folks with class privilege invented to separate themselves from what they called poor "white trash." On the surface, at least, it made the lives of racist poor white people better to have a group they could lord it over, and the only group they could lord it over were black people. Assailed and assaulted by privileged white folks, they transferred their rage and class hatred onto the bodies of black people.

Unlike the stereotypes projected by the dominant culture about poor black folks, class stereotypes claimed poor whites were supposedly easily spotted by skin ailments, bad dental hygiene, and hair texture. All these things are affected by diet. While poor southern black folks often had no money, they usually had homegrown food to eat. Poor whites often suffered from malnutrition. Living under racial apartheid, black children learned to fear poor whites more than other whites simply because they were known to express their racism by cruel and brutal acts of violence. And even when white folks with class privilege condemned this violence, they could never openly oppose it, for to do so they would have had to take the word of black folks over those of white folks, thus being disloyal to white supremacy. A white person of privilege opposing violence against blacks perpetuated by poor whites might easily ruin their reputation and risk being seen as a "nigger lover."

When I was a small child we lived in the hills without neighbors nearby. Our closest neighbors were "white trash," as distinct from poor whites. White trash were different because they flaunted their poverty, reveled in it, and were not ashamed. Poor whites, like poor blacks, were committed to trying to find work and lay claim to respectability—they were law abiding and patriotic. White trash saw themselves as above the law and as a consequence they were dangerous. White trash were folks who, as our neighbors were fond of saying, "did not give a good goddamn." They were not afraid to take the Lord's name in vain. Most poor white folks did not want to live anywhere near black folks. White trash lived anywhere. Writing in the anthology *White Trash: Race and Class in America,* Constance Penly comments in "Crackers and Whackers": "A Southern white child is required to learn that white trash folks are the lowest of the low because socially and economically they have sunk so far that they might as well be black. As such, they are seen to have lost all self-respect. So it is particularly unseemly when they appear to shamefully flaunt their trashiness, which, after all, is nothing but an aggressively in-your-face reminder of stark class difference . . . . "Privileged-class southern white folks sometimes saw white trash as more disgusting than black folks, but at the end of the day they lived by the creed that white stands with white and white makes its right.

Our "hillbilly white trash" neighbors lived by their own codes and rules. We did not call them names, because we knew the pain of slurs. Mama made it clear that they were people just like us and were to be shown respect. While they did not bother us and we did not bother them, we feared them. I never felt that they feared us. They were always encouraging us to come over, to play and party with them. To most respectable black people, poor whites and white trash were the lowest of the low. Even when they were nice, black folks felt it was important to keep a distance. I remember being whipped for being overly friendly with poor white neighbors. At that time I did not understand, nor did our parents make it clear, that if anything had happened to us in their homes, as black folks we would just have been seen as in the wrong; that was the nature of Jim Crow justice. While we were encouraged to keep a distance from all white children no matter their class, it was clear that black people pitied and often felt contempt toward the white poor.

Desegregation led to the closing of all black schools. Busing took us out of our all-black neighborhoods into worlds of whiteness we did not know. It was in high school that I first began to understand class separation between whites. Poor white kids kept to themselves. And many of their well-to-do white peers would rather be seen talking to a black person than speaking to the white poor, or worse, to white trash. There was no danger that the black person they were talking to would want to come and hang out at their home or go to a movie. Racial lines were not crossed outside school. There could be no expectation of a reciprocal friendship. A privileged white person might confuse the issue if they showed attention to an underprivileged white peer. Class boundaries had to remain intact so that no one got the wrong idea. Between black and white there was no chance of a wrong idea: the two simply did not meet or mix.

Since some folks saw mama's family as backwoods, as black hillbil-
lies, she was always quick to punish any act of aggression on our part
toward an underdog group. We were not allowed to ridicule poor
whites—not even if they were taunting us. When we began to ride
the bus across town to the white school, it was a shock to my sensibil-
ities to interact with black children who were scornful of the misfor-
tune of others. In those days it was a mark of pride for poor whites
not to take the bus. That would have placed them in a context where
black folks were in the majority. Now the white trash children of single mothers had to take the bus or walk.

To this day I have sad memories of the way Wilma, the white girl
who was in my class, was treated by aggressive black children on the
bus. Their daily taunts reminded her that she was poor white trash,
the lowest of the low, that she smelled bad, that she wore the same
dress day after day. In loud mean talk they warned her not to sit next
to them. She often stood when there was an empty seat. A big girl
with dark hair and unusually fair skin, she endured all the taunts with
a knowing smirk. When she was pushed too far she fought back. She
knew that with the exception of her ten minutes on that predominately black bus, white power ruled the day. And no matter how poor
she was, she would always be white.

Academics writing about class often make light of the racial privilege of the white poor. They make it seem as though it is merely
symbolic prestige. This is especially true of northerners. They have
no intimate knowledge of the way southern poor whites terrorize
and harass black folks in everyday life. My mother's mother lived
across town in a big old house in a white section. She could live there
because she was surrounded by the homes of poor whites. When we,
her grandchildren, were sent to see her, we feared our walk through
the poor white neighborhoods. We feared the white folks who sat on
their porches making fun of us or calling to us to "come there." We
had been told to keep our eyes straight ahead and keep on walking. In
the apartheid south, as in most northern neighborhoods, white was

always right. Poor whites knew the power race privilege gave them and they used it. Describing her background growing up in Oklahoma, Roxanne Dunbar writes of poor whites: "In the end the only advantage for most has been the color of their skin and white supremacy, particularly toward African-Americans. . . ." Race privilege has consistently offered poor whites the chance of living a better life in the midst of poverty than their black counterparts.

The white poor make up the vast majority of the poor in this society. Whereas mass migration of poor blacks from southern states to northern cities created a huge urban poor population, the white poor continue to live in isolated rural and suburban areas. Now and then they live hidden in the midst of white affluence. From their invention to the present day, the world of trailer park homes has been the territory of the white poor. While marking class boundaries, trailer park communities do not carry the stigma of degradation and deprivation commonly associated with the "ghetto"—a term first used to identify poor white urban immigrant communities. Indeed, in the not so distant past the psychological and economic self-esteem of the white working class and the white poor has been significantly bolstered by the class politics of white supremacy. Currently, we are witnessing a resurgence of white supremacist thinking among disenfranchised classes of white people. These extremist groups respond to misinformation circulated by privileged whites that suggests that black people are getting ahead financially because of government policies like affirmative action, and they are taught to blame black folks for their plight.

While anti-black racism has intensified among whites of all classes in recent years as part of civil rights backlash, overall the white underprivileged are less inclined to blame black folks for their economic plight than in the past. They are far more likely to see immigrants as the group taking needed jobs. Their racism toward nonwhite immigrants who are perceived to be taking jobs by virtue of their willingness to work for less mirrors that of black workers who blame immigrants. More and more the white and black poor recognize that ruling class greed ensures their continued exploitation and oppression.

These changes in the way the poor think are a direct result of racial integration. In many parts of the United States, desegregation led to greater contact between the black and white poor. Housing projects that had been at one time racially segregated were integrated. Greater societal acceptance of interracial bonding created the social context for white and black poor to mingle in ways unheard of at previous moments in our nation. Of course, in many areas, especially northern white cities, it was precisely this disruption of the conventional racial boundaries that led to reentrenchment along racial lines. New York and Boston ethnic white neighborhoods, where there is a class mix, remain race-segregated because racial discrimination in housing, work, etc., continues to be a norm. White power patriarchal violence is deployed daily to keep racial purity—to keep black folks, and any nonwhite group out. This does not change the fact that nowadays there is far more communication and bonding between the white and black poor.

More and more Americans of all colors are entering the ranks of the poor. And that includes white Americans. The evidence is in the numbers. In the essay "Trash-O-Nomics," Doug Henwood states what should be obvious but often is not: "Of course, the average white person is better off than the average non-white person, those of Asian origin excepted, and black people are disproportionally poor. But that sort of formula hides as much as it reveals: most officially poor people are white, and these days, a white household should consider itself lucky if its income is only stagnant rather than in outright decline." It serves white supremacist capitalist patriarchal ruling class interests to mask this reality. Hence, the almost invisibility of the white poor in mass media.

Today, most folks who comment on class acknowledge that poverty is seen as having a black face, but they rarely point to the fact that this representation has been created and sustained by mass media. Concurrently, reports using statistics that show a huge percentage of black folks in the ranks of the poor compared to a small percentage of whites make it seem that blacks are the majority group in the ranks of the poor. Rarely do these reports emphasize that these percentages are based on population size. The reality they mask is that blacks are a small percentage of the population. While black folks disproportionate to our numbers are among the poor, the vast majority of the poor continue to be white. The hidden face of poverty in the United States is the untold stories of millions of poor white people.

Better to have poor and working-class white folks believe white supremacy is still giving them a meaningful edge than to broadcast the reality that the poor of any race no longer have an edge in this society, or that downsizing daily drags previously economically sound white households into the ranks of the poor. Clearly white skin privilege makes it easier for the white poor to receive levels of support that are not accorded darker-skinned groups, whether black, Hispanic, or Asian. Undue media focus on poor nonwhites deflects attention away from the reality of white poverty.

Ruling class interests have a stake in reinforcing a politics of white supremacy, which continues to try to socialize white working-class and poor people to blame their economic plight on black people or people of color globally. Since anti-black racism has never been eliminated in the culture, it does not take much effort on the part of the dominant white supremacist capitalist patriarchal culture to brainwash poor whites to believe that it is black folks who stand in the way of their academic advancement. White hatred of nonwhite nonblack immigrants is not as virulent and intense as the hatred of black folks. As white political scientist Andrew Hacker documents in *Two Nations: Black and White, Separate, Hostile, Unequal,* in this society racism is at its most violent and dehumanizing when it comes to black folks.

No doubt ruling class groups will succeed in new efforts to divide and conquer, but the white poor will no longer direct its class rage solely at black people, for the white poor is divided within its ranks. Just as there are many poor whites who are racist, there are a substantial group of poor whites who refuse to buy into white supremacist politics, who understand the economic forces that are crippling the American working class. Progressive white poor and working-class people understand the dynamics of capitalism. All over the United States class unrest is mounting. Since there is no collective resistance the future of class struggle is not clear.

Ending welfare will mean that more white women than ever before in our nation's history will enter the ranks of the underclass. Like their black counterparts, many of them will be young. Workfare programs, which pay subsistence wages without the backdrop of free housing, will not enhance their lives. As the future "poorest of the poor" they are far less likely to be duped into believing their enemies are other economically disadvantaged groups than their predecessors. Since they are the products of a consumer-oriented culture of narcissism, they are also more inclined to be indifferent to their neighbors' plight. Constant deprivation creates stress, anxiety, along with material woes. But their desire to ease their pain can change indifference into awareness and awareness into resistance.

Given that today's culture is one where the white and black working class and poor have more to say to one another, there is a context for building solidarity that did not exist in the past. That solidarity cannot be expressed solely through shared critique of the privileged. It must be rooted in a politics of resistance that is fundamentally anti-racist, one that recognizes that the experiences of underprivileged white folks are as important as those of people of color. The class segregation that historically divided the white poor from their more privileged counterparts did not exist in predominately black communities. And while generations of white families have historically remained poor, a host of black folks pulled themselves out of poverty into privilege. In solidarity these folks have historically been strong advocates for the black poor even though that too is changing. More often than not they did not encourage solidarity with the white poor because of persistent anti-black racism. Now they must become advocates for the white and black poor, overcoming their anti-white prejudices. Concurrently, the black and white poor must do the work of building solidarity by learning more about one another, about what brings them together and what tears them apart. We need to hear more from all of us who have bridged the gap between white and black poor and working-class experience.

When I left the segregated world of my poor and working-class home environment to attend privileged-class schools, I found I often had more in common with white students who shared a similar class background than with privileged class black students who had no experience of what it might mean to lack the funds to do anything they wanted to do. No matter our color, students from poor and working-class backgrounds had common experiences history had not taught us how to sufficiently name or theoretically articulate. While it was definitely easier for folks from poor white backgrounds to assimilate visually, we all experienced estrangement from our class origin as well as the fear of losing touch with the worlds we had most intimately known. The bonds we forged in solidarity were and are not documented. There is no record of our conversations or how these solidarities shaped our future politics. Many of us used this bonding through class across the boundary of race as a groundwork for a politics of solidarity that has stood the test of time.

While racism remains an integral fact of our culture, it too has changed. Xenophobia more so than racial hatred often characterizes where white citizens stand on race. The utterly segregated black neighborhoods of my upbringing are no more. The white poor in need of shelter move into places where once no white face was ever seen. This contact does not mean an absence of racism. But it does mean that the criteria and the expression of racism has changed. It also means that there is more of a concrete basis for positive interaction between poor black and white folks. When I walk in these communities created by class division, I see grown white and black folks refusing to interact with each other even as I see more interaction than in the past. And I see white and black children freely crossing the boundaries of race to meet at that class juncture which brings them together in a common landscape they call home.

These bonds may mean little given the fact that there are so many more race-segregated white working-class and poor communities. Even in the places where white and black do not meet, there are more diverse opinions about class and race. Nothing is as simple as it was in the past when the needs of the white poor were pitted against the needs of the black poor. Today, poverty is both gendered and racialized. It is impossible to truly understand class in the United States today without understanding the politics of race and gender. Ultimately, more than any previous movement for social justice, the struggle to end poverty could easily become the civil rights issue with the broadest appeal—uniting groups that have never before taken a stand together to support their common hope of living in a more democratic and just world—a world where basic necessities of life are available to everyone, to each according to their need.

11

Solidarity with the Poor

When the musical *Jesus Christ Superstar* was staged, it included a scene in which Jesus is asked to justify the existence of poverty in a bountiful universe. He responds by declaring that "the poor will be with us always." We live in a bountiful universe and yet more than thirty-eight million live in poverty in the midst of abundance. Nowadays Jesus's declaration is a common truism. While some of us believe that poverty need not exist, we know that in our nation there is no collective commitment to ending poverty. We do what we can daily to create a culture of communalism. Our work includes both protracted struggle to end poverty and immediate effort to end the suffering poverty produces.

The poor suffer more intensely now than ever before in our nation's history. They suffer both the pain caused by material lack and all the problems it produces and the pain caused by ongoing assault on their self-esteem by privileged classes. This assault takes the form of contemptuous treatment in all walks of everyday life, of mass media representing the poor as always and only a criminal class, and most recently extreme segregation of the poor and indigent in isolated areas that are state-legitimized concentration camps.

Growing up among the poor, I and everyone in our community were taught mainly through the church that the poor were God's chosen people—that poverty should not be a cause of shame. These teachings promoted respect for the poor. Concurrently, we were socialized by our religious faith to believe that we were all responsible for the fate of those less fortunate. Offering respect and assuming accountability did not change the reality that no one wanted to be poor. And despite religious teachings, more often than not, the poor were embarrassed by their neediness. That embarrassment became shame only when the poor were treated with contempt and hostility by those more fortunate.

When I was growing up, most people believed that the poor had lives full of hardship, but rightfully we saw the poor as victims of an economic system that did not create structures to enable all citizens to adequately provide for themselves and their families. In those days, I never heard anyone suggest that people wanted to be poor. In our all-black neighborhoods, individuals who depended on state aid to survive were pitied. No one believed that they, or anyone else, wanted to be on welfare. No matter how much the church taught us about God's love of the poor, no one we knew consciously chose to live in poverty.

In our neighborhoods black folks rightly understood that the poverty in our lives was a direct consequence of post-slavery racial discrimination first in the educational system and then in employment. Deprived of equal access to adequate job preparation as well as being denied entry if one were lucky enough to be adequately prepared, black people knew that it served the interests of white supremacy to keep us poor and needy. Everyone understood this. It created a sympathetic climate where resources were shared and the poor were more often than not able to survive with their dignity and self-respect intact. While the myriad ways that racism prevented black people from collectively attaining economic self-sufficiency were openly talked about in our southern communities, no one talked about predatory capitalism. It was not common knowledge that capitalism required surplus labor, that there would always be more workers than available jobs. In fact, most black folks naively believed that if racism and the job discrimination it condoned ended, there would be jobs for everyone.

By the end of the sixties, after civil rights and black power struggle had gained for black folks more rights within the existing unequal social structure, everyone knew better. Legalized desegregation and anti-discrimination laws did not create the utopian work world of endless opportunity. While more black people entered the workforce and were able to garner fairer wages than in the past, a huge mass of black people without appropriate education and skills lingered on the bottom. State aid administered to women with children and the elderly provided meager resources. But the vast majority of unemployed poorly educated black males had no strategies to improve their chances of employment.

As more and more black people entered the ranks of the poor, as being on welfare became more an accepted norm and it was no longer deemed shameful to have children outside marriage, overall attitudes toward the poor began to change in our society. The poor were represented as predatory by the government, as wanting handouts rather than jobs. The poor were seen as using the resources of the more affluent to sustain their laziness and unproductive lifestyles. Negative stereotypes about the poor were deliberately evoked by politicians to diminish commitments to social welfare, and the accountability of the privileged was no longer expressed primarily in closed settings where public policy was formed and aid distributed; they were expressed through mass media. By the early seventies, the entire nation was being socialized via mass media to see the poor as parasites and predators whose ongoing need would make it impossible for anyone to have a good life. Hence it was deemed crucial for the survival of privileged classes to turn their backs on the poor.

The culture of communalism, which had once enabled many poor people to cope with material hardship in a dignified manner, was eroded by mainstream insistence that affluence determined value and that sharing resources only made the problem worse. Among the poor, sharing could no longer be a core value when folks began to embrace notions of liberal individualism along with the notion that one's value was determined by the ownership of things. In a world where one's ability to consume and the objects acquired determine one's worth, there can be no respect for the poor. The citizenship of consumption has no place for those who lack the power to acquire. As the values of the culture changed, so did the fate of the poor.

By the end of the seventies, to be poor was always and only a cause for shame. Gone was any attempt to talk about the poor as the chosen ones. It is no accident that attitudes toward the poor became more negative during the years when poor people developed a political voice, when they used their power to engage in strategic acts of resistance. Attacking the self-esteem of the poor was an act of sabotage. The goal was disempowerment. That attack began with the proliferation in mass media of negative stereotypes about folks receiving welfare. Even though many more white citizens were welfare recipients than black folks, the image white mass media projected was one of predatory black folks living high on the hog off the taxpayers' dollars. Single females with children were most viciously attacked. Hence a combined racist/sexist narrative surfaced that allowed non-progressive white folks of all classes to see themselves as the economic victims of needy black folks stealing their resources.

Yet this assault on the poor would not have been effective without the widespread embrace of hedonistic consumerism on the part of the poor. Acquiring material objects that bring status was offered to the poor and underprivileged as an antidote to the "shame" of poverty. In poor communities this shift began with clothing. One could live in poverty, lack a well-balanced diet, but come out of the house or welfare project wearing expensive fashions. Since clothes are a basic necessity, it was easy for poor people to fall prey to advertising in mass media that suggested that upgrading one's appearance was equivalent to changing one's class status. The only booming economy in poor communities that allows folks to consume material objects that are not basic necessities, that provides individuals with the cash needed to purchase luxury items is the drug industry. Tragically, the politics of drug profiteering and the ongoing addiction it produces creates and perpetuates a predatory violent culture.

While the working class, poor, and indigent use drugs to ease pain and numb sorrow, to feel intense pleasure however fleeting, addiction erodes self-esteem and personal integrity. Contrary to negative stereotypes which continually depict the poor as immoral, it is precisely the moral conscience of the poor that leads to shame and lowered self-esteem both among those who are addicted and those who are codependent with them. On television news, fictional cop shows, or in newpapers accounts, we do not hear stories about poor people killing each other to attain basic necessities like food, shelter, and health care. Poverty has not transformed poor communities into predatory war zones; this destabilization has been the direct result of a drug culture the nation-state condones.

Were the government interested in destroying drug cartels in the United States and creating stability in poor communities, it could easily do so. However, drugs keep the poor in their place; they keep the poor from organizing and using their class power, however relative, to challenge and change society. For example: Poor people have the right to vote. That is a form of class power. Imagine the impact 60 percent of the thirty-eight million poor people who can vote could have in any election. Or what if poor communities were organized in a communalist manner so that barter and trade could help sustain individuals in need. These are just a few examples. Yet if people are too busy getting high on abusive substances to care about politics or basic survival, the powerful public voice of resistance that

surfaced in the past among working-class and poor people demand-
ing justice will never surface again—it will not be heard.

Next to drug addiction, the recent force that has most destabilized
and devastated poor communities and families is widespread addiction to gambling. The most accepted form of gambling is playing the
lottery. While mass media highlights the rare poor individuals who
become rich instantly from winning the lottery, it ignores the masses
of needy folks who spent money that could be used for food, shelter,
or paying the bills to play the lottery instead. More than any other
addiction, gambling with the lottery fuels the fantasy that without
effort the poor can leave poverty behind and change the meaning and
value of their lives.

Nowadays, a vast majority of our nation's poor believe that you
are what you can buy. Since they can buy little they see themselves as
nothing. They have passively absorbed the assumption perpetuated by
ruling class groups that they cannot live lives of peace and dignity in
the midst of poverty. Believing this they feel no hope, which is why
folks with class privilege can label them nihilistic. Yet this nihilism is a
response to a lust for affluence that can never be satisfied and that was
artificially created by consumer culture in the first place. In the intro-
duction to *Freedom of Simplicity,* Richard Foster states: "Contemporary culture is plagued by the passion to possess. The unreasoned
boast abounds that the good life is found in accumulation, that 'more
is better.' Indeed, we often accept this notion without question, with
the result that the lust for affluence in contemporary society has
become psychotic: it has completely lost touch with reality." Nihilism
is a direct consequence of the helplessness and powerlessness that
unrelenting class exploitation and oppression produce in a culture
where everyone, no matter their class, is socialized to desire wealth—
to define their value, if not the overall meaning of their lives by material status.

The result of this psychosis for the poor and underprivileged is
despair. In the case of the black poor, that nihilism intensified because

the combined forces of race and class exploitation and oppression make it highly unlikely that they will be able to change their lives or acquire even the material objects they believe would give their lives meaning. In the past few years, I have been stunned by the way in which unrealistic longing for affluence blinds the folks I know and care about who are poor, so they do not see the resources they have and might effectively use to enhance the quality of their lives. They are not unusual. Fantasizing about a life of affluence stymies many poor people. Underprivileged folks often imagine that the acquisition of a material object will change the quality of their lives. And when it does not, they despair. In my own family I have seen loved ones fixate on a new car or a used car that is seen as a status object, pouring all their hard-earned money into this acquisition while neglecting material concerns that, if addressed, could help them change their lives in the long run.

I am thankful to have been born into a world where being poor did not mean that one was doomed to an unhappy life of despair. Yet the vast majority of the black poor today (many of whom are young) lack the oppositional consciousness that our ancestors utilized to endure hardship and poverty without succumbing to dehumanization. For the most part, today's poor lack the class consciousness that would shield them from embracing the notion that one's value is determined by material goods. In the neighborhoods of my growing up, wise black elders, many of whom had never had salaried jobs, shared their understanding that we are more than our material needs and possessions. They created lives of dignity and integrity in the midst of unrelenting hardship. They were able to do this because they refused to buy into the belief that acquiring material possessions is the only act that gives life meaning.

Our nation is not striving to eliminate the conditions that create poverty. And while we need strategies of resistance that put in place structures that will enable everyone to have access to basic necessities, in the meantime we must work to resist the dehumanization of the poor. Hope must come not through unrealistic fantasies of affluence but rather through learning ways to cope with economic hardship that do not dehumanize the poor and make it impossible for them to change their lot when opportunities arise. There are poor people dwelling in the affluent communities where I live. They are usually white. Mostly they try to hide their poverty—to blend in. Many of them are elderly and remain in the community because their housing is affordable through rent stabilization. Some of them are young people, single parents, who have been lucky enough to find affordable small living spaces in affluent neighborhoods where they feel their children will have a better chance. These folks live happy successful lives even though they are poor, just as some individuals in poor communities who lack material resources live happy lives. But it is harder to be poor when affluence is the norm all around you.

Their way of life is the concrete experience that gives the lie to all the negative stereotypes and assumptions about poverty that suggest that one can never be poor and have a happy life. They offer a vision of a good life despite poverty akin to the one I saw in my childhood. They survive by living simply—by relying at times on the support and care of more privileged friends and comrades. They may work long hours but still not have enough money to make ends meet. Yet they do not despair. Were they seduced by mainstream advertising to desire and consume material objects that are way beyond their means, they would soon destroy the peace of their lives. Were they to daily bombard their psyches with fantasies of a good life full of material affluence, they would lose touch with reality—with the good to be found in the lives that they most intimately know. And this psychic estrangement would make them unable to cope effectively with the realities of what any poor person must do to enhance their economic well-being.

Poor people who see meaning and value only in affluence and wealth can have no self-respect. They cannot treasure the good that may exist in the world around them. They live in fantasy and as a consequence are more vulnerable to acting out (overspending, stealing, buying something frivolous when they lack food). All these actions take away their power and leave them feeling helpless.

Given the reality that the world's resources are swiftly dwindling because of the wastefulness of affluent cultures, the poor everywhere who are content with living simply are best situated to offer a vision of hope to everyone, for the day will come when we will all have to live with less. If people of privilege want to help the poor, they can do so by living simply and sharing their resources. We can demand of our government that it eliminate illegal drug industries in poor neighborhoods. Imagine how many poor communities would be transformed if individuals from these communities, with help from outsiders, were given full-time jobs in the neighborhoods they lived in, employment created in the interest of making safe, drug-free environments. That could be a new industry.

Obviously, the culture of consumerism must be critiqued and challenged if we are to restore to the poor of this nation their right to live peaceful lives despite economic hardship. The poor and the affluent alike must be willing to surrender their attachment to material possessions, to undergo a conversion experience that would allow them to center their lives around nonmarket values. Affluent folk who want to share resources should be able to support a poor family for a year and write that off their taxes. Not only would this help to create a better world for us all (since none of our lifestyles are safe when predatory violence becomes a norm), it would mean that we embrace anew the concept of interdependency and accountability for the collectiveness of all citizens that is the foundation of any truly democratic and just society.

The poor may be with us always. Yet this does not mean that the poor cannot live well, cannot find contentment and fulfillment. Clearly when individuals lack food, water, shelter, these immediate needs are more pressing and should be met. But satisfying needs of the spirit are just as essential for survival as are material needs. A poor person who has hope that their life will change, that they can live a good life despite material hardship, will be a productive citizen capable of working to create the condition where poverty is no longer the norm. Without a fundamental core belief that we are always more than our material possessions, we doom the poor to a life of meaningless struggle. This is a form of psychic genocide. To honor the lives of the poor, we need to resist such thinking. We need to challenge psychic assaults on the poor with the same zeal deployed to resist material exploitation.

Solidarity with the poor is not the same as empathy. Many people feel sorry for the poor or identify with their suffering yet do nothing to alleviate it. All too often people of privilege engage in forms of spiritual materialism where they seek recognition of their goodness by helping the poor. And they proceed in the efforts without changing their contempt and hatred of poverty. Genuine solidarity with the poor is rooted in the recognition that interdependency sustains the life of the planet. That includes the recognition that the fate of the poor both locally and globally will to a grave extent determine the quality of life for those who are lucky enough to have class privilege. Repudiating exploitation by word and deed is a gesture of solidarity with the poor.

All over the world, folks survive without material plenty as long as their basic necessities are met. However, when the poor and indigent are deprived of all emotional nurturance, they cannot lead meaningful lives even if their minimal material needs are met. Visionary thinkers and leaders who are poor must be at the forefront of a mass-based movement to restore to the poor their right to meaningful lives despite economic hardship. Real life examples and testimony will serve as the primary examples that poverty need not mean dehumanization. We need to bear witness. Those of us who are affluent, in solidarity with the underprivileged, bear witness by sharing resources, by helping to develop strategies for self-actualization that strengthen the self-esteem of the poor. We need concrete strategies and programs that address material needs in daily life as well as needs of the spirit.

12

Class Claims:
Real Estate Racism

More than ever before in our nation's history, white citizens who usually refuse to talk openly about class, occasionally willingly evoke class to deflect attention away from their sustained commitment to discriminatory housing practices that bolster white supremacy. When I began seeking to buy "real estate" in Greenwich Village in New York City, telling the agents (all of whom were white) that I wanted to be in a racially diverse building, as I did not want myself or the folks coming to see me to be subjected to racism, they kept insisting that the issue was not about race but class. If buildings and neighborhoods were all white then that had more to do with class than white supremacy. Of course, whenever property that was available before we showed up and mysteriously sold by the time we arrived (and all the white parties had taken a good look at my black skin), the explanations about class wore thin.

Yet none of the agents were willing to name the reality of racism or white supremacy. Finally, in the West Village, I found a building with eleven flats where there was already a black woman who owned her place. An elderly woman who had been living in the Village for more than fifty years, she had many stories about racism and housing. Since one cannot buy into co-ops without the approval of the board, who represent the building, I asked her if the issue of race had come up at the meeting where my application was looked at. She responded by stating: "Oh Yes! Somebody mentioned your being black. And I stopped them right in their tracks. Looked them dead in the eye and told them 'she's got the money—she's just as white as the rest of you.'" In her mind, class power enables one to transcend race. In actuality had she not been a long-standing resident in the building, who had confronted racial discrimination in housing as a young woman, white supremacist thinking might have led white residents to refuse to accept applications by black people.

In the United States, racial apartheid is maintained and institutionalized by a white dominated real estate market. It never ceases to amaze me that New York City is one of the most ethnically diverse cities in the world, yet racial and ethnic segregation continues to inform housing practices both in terms of the neighborhoods individuals choose to live in, who landlords rent property to, and who is able to buy. Developing a close relationship with a white female real estate agent, I was not surprised to learn that agents initially tend to share information about select properties by word of mouth, rather than ads in newspaper or in listings that are available to the public. This behind-the-scenes sharing creates an easy context for racial discrimination to take place with no one the wiser.

In New York City when looking to buy a flat in co-ops or condos I found that it was a market shaped by white realtors (most of whom have not divested of white supremacist thinking) and white residents who were equally invested in keeping what was repeatedly termed "undesirable elements" out of their buildings. All too often undesirable means people of color, native born, and immigrant nonwhites. White residents who might ordinarily in their daily lives see themselves as "liberal" when it comes to the issue of race often acted in a conservative manner when it came to allowing blacks/people of color into their building. As a single woman professional seeking rental housing in buildings, I was often told by residents that I was acceptable but the individuals who might visit me might be undesirable. When I pressed them to identify who these individuals might be, I was told that black males were in this category.

Contrary to the notion that class power allows one to transcend race in the arena of real estate, liberals and conservatives alike tend to evoke class to justify racism. Folks will insist that they are not racist, then simultaneously argue that everyone knows property values will diminish if too many black people enter the neighborhood. They may even say that while they do not agree with this policy they collude in upholding it to maintain property values. In Andrew Hacker's book *Two Nations: Black and White, Separate, Hostile, Unequal,* he documents that laws forbidding racial discrimination in housing have had little impact. Studies indicate that while an overwhelming majority of black people would prefer to live in mixed neighborhoods, most white people prefer segregated neighborhoods or accept racial integration if it means one black person or family lives in their area. Hacker documents that irrespective of their political beliefs, hardly any white folks choose to live in an area where half or more of the residents are blacks. And in those cases where black people move into a predominately white neighborhood, if our presence exceeds 8 percent, whites usually leave and no new white people move in. Hacker explains: "What makes integration difficult if not impossible is that so few whites will accept even a racial composition reflecting the overall national proportion of 12 or 13 percent." Acknowledging that many whites support racial integration in principle, Hacker calls attention to the reality that, in practice, most white people support segregation.

Attempting to deflect attention from the extent to which white supremacist thinking shapes notions of who we should live with and among, Hacker suggests that discrimination in housing often has "more to do with culture or class." He writes: "White people themselves vary in income and other signals of status, and every section of the nation has hierarchies among white neighborhoods. Even in an area where everyone earns essentially the same income, many residents would not want a homosexual on their block, or neighbor who parks a business van (PARAGON PEST CONTROL) in his driveway every night. Simply being a fellow white is not enough to make a person a desired neighbor." Of course, whites cannot simply look at other white people who want to rent or buy in their neighborhood and know if they are gay or what type of vehicle they may park in their driveway. Hacker undercuts his own argument about class when he proceeds to document the reality that whites move out of neighborhoods when the black proportion reaches somewhere between 10 and 20 percent, even when the black people moving in have the same economic and social standing or higher.

No matter how many times white people are told that they are more likely to be robbed or assaulted by someone of their race, many white people still evoke fear of crime to explain their class-based racism when it comes to the issue of housing. And again when the black people moving into their neighborhood are economically well-off and share a similar economic standing, they then project that it is the folks who come to visit them who represent a potential threat. Ironically, of course, there are many upper-class fancy white neighborhoods tyrannized by crimes perpetrated by white folks, yet this fact does not change property values or lead these residents to distrust all white people. Hacker documents the reality that class-based white supremacy leads all people of color to be seen as undesirable elements, but especially black people.

In a society like ours where class is rarely, if ever, talked about, it is worthy of note that whenever racism in real estate and housing is talked about, most white people will argue that discrimination is really about class rather than race. My most progressive white friends and acquaintances refuse to acknowledge that white supremacist thinking rules when it comes to real estate. They would rather believe white folks are only protecting property values rather than perpetuating and reinforcing white supremacy. Hacker writes: "Americans have extraordinarily sensitive antennae for the coloration of white neighborhoods. In virtually every metropolitan area, white householders can rank each enclave by the racial makeup of the residents. Given this knowledge, where a family lives becomes an index of its social standing. While this is largely an economic matter, proximity to black compounds this assessment. For a white family to be seen as living in a mixed—or changing—neighborhood can be construed as a symptom of surrender, indeed as evidence that they are on a downward spiral." In the United States, one's class standing then is always determined by racial factors as well as economic factors. An all-black upper-class neighborhood rarely has the same class standing as an all-white upper-class neighborhood, nor is the property valued the same. Most of the white people working in real estate whom I interviewed or talked with informally refused to acknowledge the impact racial discrimination and white supremacy have when it comes to housing. Again and again they tried to insist that the issue was class, not race, refusing to acknowledge that the two systems are utterly enmeshed when it comes to real estate. Only young white people working in real estate were willing to talk about discriminatory practices, those of agents, landlords, and homeowners.

While I have purchased homes in predominately white neighborhoods in California, Ohio, and Florida, they were all for sale by owner. With the exception of the California property, white owners expressed concern about selling their houses to a black person. In Ohio, the white couple who sold me their house were planning to remain in the same neighborhood. Before the sale, without calling, they showed up at my doorstep wanting to see where I lived. They wanted to make sure I had the appropriate "class" credentials. They were afraid their "liberal" neighbors would blame them for bringing an undesirable element into the neighborhood. Of course, these same harsh discriminatory practices are rarely deployed when the clients are white.

When I first began to look for property in Florida, I found that real estate agents were eager to show me places where the cost was already inflated. And white owners seeking to make inordinate profits were quite willing to sell to nonwhite buyers. Indeed, real estate speculation has done more to change the racial makeup of neighborhoods than laws forbidding racial discrimination or anti-racist housing practices. Inflated prices make it difficult for white flight to take place with as much ease as it once did. In many major cities, white people (and other groups) with class privilege are actually moving into areas that were once populated solely by poor and working-class groups, oftentimes nonwhite. Their class power raises rents, taxes, the cost of housing in ways that require the poor and working class to leave. Without overt expressions of class antagonism or racial conflict, the poor are forced out by a class mobility that they cannot intervene on. This happens as well in small towns. The small town where I bought my house has a large population of black people and had at one time a thoroughly racially integrated community. But as more white people with money came to the area raising both property taxes and the cost of housing, better neighborhoods became increasingly all white. This type of shift often occurs in college towns where there is a liberal white constituency who want to find affordable housing and to live in a racially/ethnically mixed environment.

In a state where land is scarce, poor communities are often "colonized" by upwardly mobile unconventional young whites from privileged-class backgrounds who are willing to move into areas whites once avoided. One can easily document changes in real estate in major cities (for example, San Francisco, Oakland, Berkeley), where areas that once were poor and nonwhite are infiltrated by nonconventional whites from privileged-class backgrounds (in the Bay area the search for communities less hostile to gay inhabitants led many young whites to poorer, nonwhite neighborhoods). When these groups pay higher rents than the poor and working-class people who were there before them, neighborhoods change. Entire areas in San

Francisco that were historically black and Hispanic are now white. They were changed by a convergence of real estate speculation, class elitism, and white supremacist thinking.

The changes in real estate in New York City are even more evident. Mary Barfoot documents the class and race politics informing these shifts in *Bottom Fish Blues: The Coming of Black Genocide*. Her analysis of the way Harlem is slowly becoming a nonblack world remains insightful. She contends: "Harlem sits on top of Manhattan and was the seed-bed of Afrikan-American rebellion. So let's cut off the head kill the snake. Harlem is to become white man's land. Every year there is less and less housing for poor Afrikan-Americans and Latinas. This is the plan, a long range plan by the white ruling class and carried out by the Koch administration. In 1974 the city took over the Semiramis and in 1978 it took over the Kido, for instance. Two large apartment buildings in central Harlem, structurally sound and over-looking the north end of Central Park. Instead of fixing them up for the homeless, the city "warehoused" the two buildings for a decade. Now the city has sold them both to developers for a mere $35,000. The state is going to loan the developers $350,000 for engineering work, and the developers promise to condo the two buildings—71 apartments for sale at $130,000-plus apiece. Not for homeless Afrikan-American women and children. The city has warehoused much of Harlem, consciously de-populating it. Their plan is for near-total Afrikan and Puerto-Rican removal from Manhattan." Barfoot published these essays in 1993; in less than ten years, the city has managed to use its control of 60 percent of the housing in Harlem to force the poor and working class out by creating a yuppie Harlem, which will soon have a large white lower- and middle-class population.

This type of state-orchestrated, racialized class warfare is taking place all around the United States. Barfoot writes: "Davis was the one Afrikan-American hangout for working people in Annapolis, Maryland's state capital. Now 'Davis' is a yuppie pub, still with the same name, where the governor dines and where Black people are not welcome. The Castro was a poor Afrikan–American and Latin neighborhood in central San Francisco. Fifteen years ago the government began helping gay white men to 'redevelop' Afrikan–Americans and Latins out, as the Castro became a special community for gay white men, their small businesses and homes." This type of shift has now helped change the racial and ethnic make-up of San Francisco. It has made the areas where people of color without class privilege are allowed to live more densely populated, more lacking in the services needed to maintain environmentally safe housing.

Significantly, Barfoot was one of the first critics of racialized class warfare in real estate to call attention to the fact that changes in the class status of white women had both negative and positive impact. She contends: "Homelessness for Afrikan–American women is directly related to white women's search for equality with white women. In particular, young white women need housing—if you're going to be independent and not living with a man, then you need your own place. White women as well as men need more and more housing." Using New York City, particularly the politics of housing in Manhattan, as an example, she calls attention to the ways in which the upwardly mobile class aspiration of white women have also been a catalyst for the displacement of people of color. Barfoot contends: "A luppie (lesbian professional) doesn't need to harm or displace a fly, but she has an apartment in what used to be 'Spanish Harlem.' A feminist doctor I know of was a brownstoning 'urban pioneer' in Brooklyn. Never noticing that she was part of the 'white tornado' ripping out women of color and their families." No studies have been done documenting the link between newly found class mobility among white women, women of color with class privilege, and the displacement of poor and working-class communities that is the result of both feminist movement and the racialized class politics of upward mobility. Dennis Altman's *The Americanization of the Homosexual: The Homosexualization of America* looks at the rising class power of white gay men (along with some men of color) and how it has changed both real estate and public policy focusing on the issues of housing.

Significantly, folks who do not see themselves as racist or prejudiced have no qualms about supporting racial discrimination if they feel that support is necessary to maintain class power. All around the United States the neighborhoods of the poor and indigent are often more diverse than is the norm because of the structure of public housing and affordable housing. Among groups with class privilege and power there is far more discrimination. The identification with property values as a source of status and economic investment is the class politics that undergirds our nation's acceptance of housing discrimination. We are one of the few countries in the world that condones the killing of individuals for trespassing on private property. The rights of those who own real estate are more protected than the rights of children and women who are victimized daily by domestic violence. In a culture where the protection of private property is sustained by a zeal akin to that evoked by religious fundamentalism, it is difficult to engage collective public support to end discrimination, to create appealing, safe, affordable housing for all.

Much of the attack on state-funded welfare has been aimed at taking away poor people's access to public housing. This has led to widespread homelessness. It is a testimony to the worship of private property that our nation does little to address the issue of homelessness. To provide housing for the homeless, citizens of this nation would have to believe that everyone has a right to shelter and that this right should be affirmed and protected by our tax dollars. Tragically, most citizens in the United States readily accept the notion that their tax dollars should support militarism that we are told will keep us safe, while ignoring the danger most people face when incomes are shrinking and affordable housing is lacking. Most citizens do not own their housing and have been lulled by the logic of capitalism to believe mortgages make them secure. As downsizing takes place in the workforce, more and more workers lose their homes.

These losses are hidden. Mass media tells us that sales of property are good, that the market is strong. It tell us that the market is strong for those who have unlimited resources.

More than any other issue facing our nation, housing will be the concern that will force citizens to face the reality of class. Every day citizens of this nation buy houses they cannot afford and will not own in their lifetime. Ironically, in many parts of our nation the houses get bigger and grander even as incomes dwindle. The gap between those who have and those who have not will be registered by the revolt of citizens who once believed that they would always have the right to own, confronting the reality that housing is rapidly becoming a luxury that only those with unlimited resources can hold on to. Anybody with credit can buy a house but not everyone can keep their home. Housing will be the site of future class struggle in this nation. As the homeless increase, as jobs are lost and homes become crowded or impossible to find and hold on to, class discrimination in housing will become more apparent. Those of us who have class privilege, who reside somewhere in the middle of our society's economic totem pole, will have to choose where we stand. Will we stand for the right of everyone to have safe affordable housing irrespective of income or will we stand with the greedy—the speculators in real estate who only exploit for profit?

Making real estate speculation work for homeowners with a degree of class privilege who are nevertheless not rich is the seduction offered those who have a degree of class privilege. It allies our class interests with that of the ruling classes who are only concerned with profit. When I was buying my house in Florida, where real estate speculation is the drug most folks are addicted to, I was continually told by realtors that I would be able to make a huge profit. I had to constantly remind them that I was looking for a home—a place to live. That while I desired to be able to sell my house for what I paid for it in the event that I needed to leave it, my primary concern was finding a home. Encouraging individuals to think of buying a home as an investment where they can make huge profits deflects our nation's attention away from the real politics of real estate. Huge profits in real estate speculation, whether on an individual or corporate level, lead to grave losses that are unseen: the folks who lose their homes daily whom we do not see, the many grown children with children taking up residence in the homes of parents because they cannot afford a place to live, the people turned away from public housing (condemned by the city then sold to developers), and the growing number of homeless citizens who live not on the street but in shelters that are like camps. The invisible pain about housing that is widespread in our nation will become more visible as the people take to the streets—to demand housing for us all—an end to dehumanizing real estate speculation, an end to discrimination.

13

Crossing Class Boundaries

Most of my formative years were spent in segregated black communities where our immediate neighbors were from diverse class backgrounds. Some folks were poor—just barely getting by and making ends meet. They lived in tiny railroad shacks and kept them neat and tidy. Then there were the working-class families like ours, with lots of hungry mouths to feed, so that even if fathers had good jobs like working in the coal mines, it could still be hard sometimes to make ends meet. If the women in these families worked they did service jobs—housecleaning, cooking, or working now and then in the tobacco fields or on the loosening floor. The lovely freshly painted houses in our neighborhood usually belonged to middle-class folks and the rare person with lots of money. They were schoolteachers, doctors, lawyers, and undertakers.

If anyone suffered economic hardship in that world somebody knew and ways were found to share—to meet needs. In that small segregated world it was hard to keep secrets. At school teachers paid attention and they knew if a child was in need. At church everyone saw you. And if all else failed somebody would come by your house and see about you. Not all neighborhoods in the town were like ours; it was a place where folks knew each other's business and often did not hesitate to put their nose in it if need be.

Our family was big, six girls, one boy, mom, and dad. Dad worked various jobs but the one he held for most of his adult life was as a janitor at the local post office. He began working this job when racial discrimination was still the norm, and white folks thought they were doing no wrong when they paid white workers a fair wage and black workers far less for doing the same job. Laws forbidding unfair practices changed this practice for those employees who worked for the state but continued in all cases where there was no system of checks and balances.

Even though dad worked hard, in our household there was never enough money because there were so many of us. Yet we never lacked the basic necessities of life. Mama cooked delicious food. We always had clean clothes. And even though the old house we lived in was expensive to heat and often cold in winter, we had shelter. We did not think about class. We thought about race. The boundaries of class could be crossed. At times class-based conflict surfaced, often over the desires middle-class schoolteachers had for their working-class and poor students that differed from parental desires. No matter our class we all lived in the same segregated world. We knew each other and we tried to live in community.

When I chose to attend a "fancy" college rather than a state school close to home, I was compelled to confront class differences in new and different ways. Like many working-class parents, my folks were often wary of the new ideas I brought into their lives from ideas learned at school or from books. They were afraid these fancy ideas like the fancy schools I wanted to attend would ruin me for living in the real world. At the time I did not understand that they were also afraid of me becoming a different person—someone who did not speak their language, hold on to their beliefs and their ways. They were working people. To them a good life was one where you worked hard, created a family, worshiped God, had the occasional good time, and lived day to day.

Even though I wanted to attend fancy schools, like the working class and poor around me, I shared these beliefs. I was not afraid to work hard. I just wanted to work in the world of ideas. That was hard for working people to understand. To them it made sense if you wanted to be a teacher because schoolteachers earned a decent living and were respected. Beyond that they could see no practical use for the learning one would get in a fancy school.

I suppose the first major class conflict of my life was my decision about where to go to college. It would have been easier for my family had I chosen to go to a state college near home where I might be awarded a full scholarship, where dorms were cheap, and required books could be checked out of libraries. I wanted to go to a fancy private college. And since my folks did not talk openly about money matters or speak freely of their fears that I would leave home and become a stranger to the world of my growing, I did not realistically consider what it would be like to cross the boundaries of class, to be the working-class girl attending the rich school. No wonder my parents feared for me and my fate. They could see what I could not see.

Against the will of my parents I decided to attend a fancy college far away from home. To attend this school I needed scholarships and loans. I had to work to buy books and there would be no coming home for the holidays because it required excess money we did not have. I wanted to attend this school because I had been told by a favorite teacher that it was a place for serious thinkers, where ideas were taken seriously. This teacher, an anti-racist white liberal who came from an upper-class background, did not talk to me about the issue of class.

It did not take long for me to understand that crossing class boundaries was not easy. My class values were not the same as my college peers'. I resented their assumptions about the poor and working class. I did not find black bourgeois elites to be any more aware of my world than their white counterparts. The few friends I made whether black or white usually came from a similar class background. Like me they worked; they had loans, scholarships. Publicly and at school I mingled with everybody, learning about different class values. Privately, in my home, whether dormitory room or cheap apartment, I nurtured the values I had been raised to believe in. I wanted to show my family and community of origin that I could go out into the world and be among more privileged class people without assimilating, without losing touch with the ground of my being.

Living among folks from more privileged classes, I learned more about class than I had ever learned in a small segregated neighborhood. Before living among upper-class and rich folks, I had never heard anyone speak contemptuously about poor and working-class people. Casual articulation of negative stereotypes stopped me in my tracks. Not only was I usually a dissenting voice about class, after a while it was just assumed that I would go my way. It was among privileged class folks that I developed both an awareness of the extent to which they are willing to go to protect their class interest and a disrespect for their class values.

Even though I was struggling to acquire an education that would enable me to leave the ranks of the poor and working class, I was more at home in that world than I was in the world I lived in. My political solidarity and allegiance was with working people. I created a lifestyle for myself that mixed aspects of my working-class background with new ideas and habits picked up in a world far removed from that world. I learned different ways to dress, different ways to eat, and new ways to talk and think. I took from those experiences what I wanted and linked them with my home training.

Confident that nothing could separate me from the world of my growing up, I crossed class boundaries with ease and grace. At home with my parents I spoke the language of our world and our ways. At school I learned to keep these ways to myself. I did not fit in and I did want to fit in. At the same time I was coming to understand that this crossing of class boundaries had indeed given me a different sense of self. I could go home again. I could blend in, but the doors to that world threatened to close whenever I tried to bring new ideas there, to change things there.

Like much of the writing I have done on class, I began this essay by telling family stories again and again, often the same stories in different ways. My ongoing connection to the working-class world of my origin has consistently served as the site of challenge and interrogation for my class values and political allegiances. Affirming and sustaining direct connections to that world continually compels me to think critically about class dynamics in this society. In my twenties it seemed a simple matter to journey between varied class experience. During those years the amount of money I made would have placed me among the ranks of the poor or bottom-level working class. But class is more than money. And the doctorate I was earning was preparation for entering the ranks of the upper-middle class.

My first full-time tenure track teaching job at a fancy school, Yale University, signaled a complete transition in class positionality. I was no longer in limbo, moving back and forth between the worlds of the haves and the have-nots. I was no longer officially a member of the working class. Like many folks from working-class and poor backgrounds, much of my salary went to the debts I had accumulated on the way. Raised by all the tenets of racial uplift to believe that it is the duty of those who get ahead to share their resources with others, especially those less fortunate, I committed myself to giving to the needy a fixed portion of my income.

Although I did not see myself as part of a talented tenth in the way DuBois first used that term, I was among the first generation in my family to go to college and the only one of us then to finish a doctorate. It had been a journey full of personal hardship and struggle. And I knew that I would never have finished without the ongoing support of the working class world I had come from. These connections were my strength. The values I had been raised to believe in sustained me when everything in the new worlds I entered invalidated me and the world I was coming from. I felt that I had both a debt and a responsibility to that world—to honor it and to remain in solidarity with it despite the change in my class position.

One way to honor this working-class world was to write about it in a way that would shed a more authentic light on our reality. I felt that writing about the constructive values and beliefs of that world would act as an intervention challenging stereotypes. Concurrently, I did not want to become one of those academics from a working-class background who nostalgically fetishized that experience, so I also wrote about the negative aspects of our life. My parents and other folks from that world refused to accept that it was important to write about negative experiences. They did not care how many positive comments were made, they felt betrayed whenever I focused on negative aspects of our lives. Not everyone felt this way, but it was still difficult to face that some of the folks I cared about the most felt I had become a traitorous outsider, looking in and down on the world I had most intimately known.

Ironically, the radical intellectual milieus I circulated in were ones where everyone talked about crossing class boundaries as though it was a simple matter. This was especially the case in feminist and cultural studies circles. To many of my peers from privileged class backgrounds, crossing boundaries often meant slumming or a willingness to go work in a poor community in an exotic foreign land. I was fascinated and oftentimes a bit envious when my white peers talked about their trips to Belize, El Salvador, New Guinea, Ecuador, all over Africa, India, China, and the Middle East; the list could go on. Sometimes these trips were about "eating the other," about privileged Westerners indulging in ethnic cultural cannibalism. At other times they were about individuals trying to learn about the experiences of people unlike themselves, trying to contribute.

Whatever the motivation, these experiences might someday serve as the cultural capital evoked to justify a lack of accountability toward the "different and disenfranchised" in one's own nation, town, community. Like a charity one has donated capital to and need never give again because the proof of generosity was already on record, their one-time contribution could take the place of any ongoing constructive confrontation with class politics in the United States. The starving in a foreign country are always more interesting than the starving who speak your language who might want to eat at your table, find shelter in your house, or share your job.

I found and find it difficult, though never impossible, to move back and forth among different classes. As I began to make more money and gain recognition as a feminist thinker and cultural critic, the money I earned became a source of conflict between me and members of my family and friends. Even though I had held different ideas from family and friends for years, when it came to making money, we were all struggling. By my mid-thirties, I was no longer struggling and my income was growing. The fact that I was single and had no children made it easier for me to pay debts and live cheaply in ways that family and friends could not. While I wanted to share economic resources with them, I also wanted to share knowledge, to share information about how we might all change our lives for the better.

Since I was not a flashy dresser or big spender in any highly visible way, less economically privileged peers often did not see me as a success. To them I was unconventional or weird. Once, my brother, who left the ranks of the middle class by overspending and substance abuse, came to visit me in my New York City flat and expressed shock that it was small and not very fancy. He shared: "I thought you had made it to the big time." And wanted to know: "Why are you living like this?" I explained that I lived a simple but to my way of thinking luxurious life so that I would have more to share with others. Still it was only when I concretely showed him the finances, how much I made, how it was spent (paying my expenses and helping others with rent, education, bills, etc.) that he began to realistically understand my perspective.

Like many lower-class and poor folk, he had an unrealistic sense of what one could actually do with money. This lack of awareness stems in part from the reality that credit and extended indebtedness allows so many people to consume beyond their means and create lifestyles that they cannot afford. I once did a workshop with a group of middle- and upper-middle-class professional black women on money and how we use it and was astonished to find that the vast majority of them were living so far beyond their means that they were just a paycheck away from having nothing. Folks who do not have economic privilege and have never had it often assume that they can measure someone's economic worth by material objects. They do not see the indebtedness that may be bolstering what appears on the surface to be a lifestyle one could create only with class privilege and affluence.

Indeed, black folk with some degree of class privilege often create a lifestyle that has the appearance of prosperity (big house, new car, fancy clothes) though they may be suffering economic distress because of assuming responsibility for less-fortunate family members while still striving to appear on top of it all. Studies show that most middle-income black folks with a sizable income give a measure of that income to help extended family and kin. It is not the giving that undermines their finances but their desire to have an expensive lifestyle as well as excess funds to help others. Stress and conflict over money may undermine the relationships that they hope to maintain and strengthen by sharing resources.

The more money I made, the more needy individuals came seeking financial help. Difficulties began to arise when frustrations about having their material needs met and my response to those frustrations prevented us from attending to the overall emotional needs of any positive relationship. And it was evident that the politics of shame around being needy made it impossible for some individuals to not feel "looked down" upon for desiring assistance even if they were not actually being looked down upon.

Money is so often used as a way to coercively assert power over others that it can easily become an arena of conflict, setting up hierarchies that were not previously present. Like many folks in my position, I often confront needy individuals who see my willingness to share as a weakness and who become exploitative. And there are times when I am scammed and misused (for example, a student says that they need money to finish school—you give the money—and they drop out, pocketing the refund, etc.). Any effort to not ally oneself with the existing structure of class elitism, to share resources, will necessarily meet with conflicts and casualties because many underprivileged folks share the predatory capitalist values often associated solely with the affluent. Often consciousness-raising has to take place with those who lack material privilege so that old models of guilt-tripping and exploiting progressive individuals who are working to live differently are not deployed.

All too often the affluent want to share using the old models of philanthropy and patronage that support giving while protecting one's class interest. This kind of giving rarely intervenes on or challenges the structures of economic class exploitation. Concurrently, affluent individuals who care about those who suffer the brunt of an unjust economic system often lose heart if their efforts to share are misused. This response can be an act of sabotage and self-indulgence. Politically astute individuals with class privilege have to remain aware that we are working with inadequate models for communalism and social change so that there will necessarily be occasions when the best efforts fail to get the desired outcome.

When I have experienced a breakdown of communication and misuse, I use it as an occasion to invent methods of intervention that will work. When sharing resources does not work, it would be simple to refuse to identify with the class-based suffering of those in need and assume a protective stance that would indicate allegiance to privileged-class interests. However, I remain committed to an anti–class elitism vision of solidarity that sees working things out and processing issues in such a way that bonds across class are strengthened as part of resistance struggle. This has not been a straightforward or an easy task. There is little theoretical or practical work written about how we must behave and what we must do to maintain solidarity in the face of class difference.

The most difficult issues I have had to face in the struggle to help underprivileged comrades create better lives for themselves surface when I challenge the ways widespread acceptance of hedonistic consumerism and its concomitant insistence that one never delay gratification undermines the class power of poor and working-class citizens. Years ago my partner at the time, who was also from a working-class background, and I bought a house. For a year we were overextended financially. When we first moved in we did not have a refrigerator. We had decided we could afford to buy one with cash a few months later and thereby reduce our indebtedness. To many of our working-class friends and family this seemed like a hardship. They did not understand our wanting to stabilize our finances before making another big purchase. Similarly, both our families had difficulty accepting our commitment to driving the same car for years so as not to incur unnecessary indebtedness.

Crossing class boundaries, entering worlds of class privilege, was one way that I learned different attitudes toward money than the ones I was raised with. Among the privileged there was much more information available about how to manage money. Taking this knowledge and sharing with folks without class privilege can be a gesture that provides them with the means to assert more meaningful agency in their financial lives. Through reading self-help books about money I learned the importance of keeping accounts, of knowing how I spent money. When I first shared this with comrades who lacked material privilege they thought it did not pertain to their lives. One of my sisters, who was receiving welfare at the time, could not see the point in using this exercise. In her mind she had no money. I called attention to the fact that she smoked cigarettes, which cost money. The important point was to know how you spent your money whether or not you had ten, fifty, or five hundred dollars a month. Taking charge by knowing what we spend money on and budgeting our money no matter the amount empowers. It gives a sense of economic agency and lays the groundwork for economic self-sufficiency.

Like many individuals who have come from poor and working-class backgrounds into class privilege, I want to share my life with folks from diverse class backgrounds, and not simply my resources. Oftentimes it is easier to share resources than it is to bring diverse class experiences together. When we do cross the boundaries there is usually a clash in etiquette, values, the way we do things. Since I want my family to have a firsthand knowledge of the work I do, I often invite them to attend conferences where I am lecturing. At one conference I felt my youngest sister, who had joined me, was behaving disrespectfully toward me. A single parent who received state aid and who was aggressively seeking employment but finding it extremely difficult, she was depressed and fearful about her future. I confronted her about her behavior in front of another academic colleague and friend. This offended her. She felt that I had asserted class power to belittle her although she did not use those terms.

While I still felt my critique was justified, I did agree that I had not chosen an appropriate moment to lodge it. I acted from the assumption that we were all mature adults together who could cope with a moment of tension and conflict. I had not considered the dynamics from the perspective of class difference. Since I work hard to not develop ego-centered attachment to my class power and status it is often easy for me to forget that it can be intimidating to others. My brother and I have had the most productive personal class conflicts because he is totally candid about his own class frustrations. Previous states of indebtedness and unemployment have made it difficult for him to gain economic stability even though he works hard. He openly voices his resentment of my class position and we are able to process together. To maintain our bond, our solidarity, is hard work. Friends from working-class backgrounds where siblings share similar income need not work as hard to maintain connection.

The fear of losing connection has led many an upwardly mobile individual from a poor or working-class background to cease their efforts to change their class status. Among people of color we see that decision to not go forward most intensely around the question of education. In the segregated schools of my growing up, to work hard at one's studies was a source of pride for the race and, though we did not understand it that way, for our class as well. That has now changed. At all educational levels students from working-class backgrounds fear losing touch with peers and family. And that fear often leads to self-sabotage. To intervene on this nonproductive pattern we do need more testimony both in oral traditions and in writing of how working-class and poor folk can remain connected to the communities of our origin even as we work to improve our economic lot. Hollywood dramatized these dimensions of class struggle in the hit movie *Good Will Hunting*. In the film, the working-class buddy persuades his blonde, blue-eyed "genius" friend to go forward and enter the corporate world and make big money even if he must leave his friends behind. Ironically, since he is supported by his poor and working-class peers there is no logical reason he must leave them behind. After showing audiences the pleasures that can be shared when people cross class boundaries (our poor boy hero has a lover girl from a rich background with a trust fund), the movie offers the age-old message that attaining money, status, and class privilege is the only thing that matters and not loyalty to friends and comrades.

Many intelligent, sometimes brilliant, young black males end up in prison precisely because they want to make the quick easy money rather than slowly with hard work and effort pull themselves up from the bottom. Their smarts are now being exploited by a booming industry that provides them jobs for little or no wages. They end up doing in prison what they were refusing to do on the outside without reaping minimal reward. In *The Seven Laws of Money*, Michael

Phillips contends: "About ninety percent of all crimes are committed because of money . . . and about eighty percent of all people in jail are there because of money related crimes. . . . Money is a very significant reason for people being in jail, . . . Maybe one way of stating it is that their aspiration for money and their ability to accumulate it are radically different. People who commit a crime often reach a state where they want money so badly that they are willing to take a higher risk than most other people are." Of course Phillips, who worked hard to acquire wealth, makes this point using examples of working-class and poor men. However, he does not acknowledge that the values shaping their actions are those appropriated from more affluent individuals, usually white, from more privileged class backgrounds who have been able to make easy money. These attitudes trickle down to the masses through media. And whether true or false they are often passively appropriated.

Like many commentators who write about money, Phillips avoids the issue of economic injustice and makes it appear that anyone who works hard can easily earn money. Even though he acknowledges that the issue for most poor and working-class people is not that they do not make money but that their fantasies of what money can do far exceed reality. It is always troubling to me when I hear individuals with class privilege assert that the poor and working class are unwilling to work hard. I am enraged when I hear black elites talk about how the poor need to learn from those who have made it how to work hard. The truth is that the working class and working poor work hard but the money that they make is not enough to provide them with the means to attain economic self-sufficiency. One of the greatest threats to their economic well-being is the prevailing fantasy that if they work hard, they can attain all that they desire.

Crossing class boundaries I find that many of the working-class and poor people I know spend an inordinate amount of time fantasizing about the power of money, of what it can do. While this may hold true for middle-class people as well, the extent to which these fantasies negatively impact on those without privilege is more apparent. Obsessive fantasizing about money to buy things not only creates psychotic lust, it prevents individuals from realistically confronting their economic reality or using the time and energy to constructively respond to the world they live in. Poverty need not mean that people cannot have reading groups, study groups, consciousness-raising groups. Time spent fantasizing might be best spent buying a can of bright paint (if the funds are available) and painting old furniture or just cleaning up.

Using the example of two smart black men who were caught up in easy money fantasies, Phillip writes: "They were such bright and charming people that they could have had a high salary in almost any conventional business. At each point, though they always wanted money instantly, not realizing they would always have gotten more money if they had just been able to wait a little . . . The main lesson that I could draw from these two men, both skilled, charming, capable people, is that they have such a completely distorted view of what they 'need' that there is no way they can function in society. A minor adjustment in their sense of reality would have made them capable of functioning in a useful, viable way." Given racial discrimination in conventional business, it would no doubt not have been as simple for these two men to succeed as Phillips makes it seem, but they certainly did not need to turn to crime. The fantasy of easy money led them astray.

Sadly, no group should know better than the working class and poor that there is no easy money to be had in this society. And yet the fantasy of easy money coupled with hedonistic consumerism has distorted reality for many people. Dialoguing across class is one of the ways that we can share together a more realistic sense of the limitations of money—of what it can and cannot do. Like the struggle to attain money, to change one's class position, if you start on the bottom rung, these conversations require courage, a willingness to speak truthfully about class and money that is the first act of resistance challenging and changing class elitism.

14

Living without Class Hierarchy

Most American citizens do not acknowledge the reality of class difference, of class exploitation, and they continue to believe that this is a classless society. What they mean by this is not that citizens do not occupy different class positions, but that these class positions are not fixed. Despite grave injustice and all the barriers that make it practically impossible to change your class position, if you are born on the bottom of this society's economic totem pole, it is still true that a teeny fraction of that population squeezes and militantly forces their way from the bottom up. And we consider ourselves fortunate, lucky, blessed. Yet from the onset of this book and throughout its pages I have endeavored to frankly share the human costs of class mobility, to identify both the pleasure and the pain of those who come from the bottom closer to the top can feel.

While the amount of money I have made in the last ten years identifies me as upper class, I do not identify with this class positionality even though I often enjoy the class power it affords me. I identify with democratic socialism, with a vision of participatory economics within capitalism that aims to challenge and change class hierarchy. I like that the money I make, which places me in an economic upper class, can be used in the service of redistribution of wealth, can be used to enhance the economic well-being of others through vigilant practices of giving and sharing.

I have written many books about injustice, about ending race, gender, and class exploitation, but this is the only book I have written that focuses directly on the issue of class. More than any other book I have written, writing it aroused in me intensities of pain that often left me doubled over my writing table, hurting to my heart, weeping. For no matter the class privilege I hold today, for most of my life I have lived as one with the poor and working classes. The class connection and unity I felt in my family of origin and with other poor and struggling folks as I made my way through graduate school and up the economic ladder affords me a constant awareness of class pain, of class yearning, and of the deep grief that is caused by a pervasive sense of class failure many poor and working-class people feel because they do not manage to earn enough, to earn more, to effectively change their economic lives so that they can know well-being.

At times when I have spoken publicly about a family member living in poverty, living for a time without electricity or phone, without enough, audience members stand to attack my privilege. Never do I explain to them that one person with one income giving aid is never enough, that the dilemmas of poor and working-class folks are caused by more than just economics, that class is more than money. I can give money. But rarely is money enough. I cannot give instant psychological makeovers. The imprints of a consumer capitalist socialization that teaches us all to spend much and value little, to get as much as we can and give as little as possible (it's known as scamming) cannot be erased at will. It should be evident that we cannot change class oppression and exploitation without changing the way everyone thinks about getting and giving. Class is much more than money. Until we understand this fact, the notion that problems in all our lives, but most especially the lives of the indigent and the poor, can be solved by money will continue to serve the interests of a predatory ruling class while rendering the rest of us powerless to create meaningful changes in our lives across class.

In these essays I have hoped to share that the pain of being without enough money to survive adequately or well, that the widening gap between the rich and the poor, causes pain far beyond economic suffering, that it rends and breaks us psychologically, tearing us asunder, denying us the well-being that comes from recognizing our need for community and interdependency. Given the huge gap between those who have a lot, those who have a little, and those who have nothing, it is difficult to understand how citizens of this nation can imagine that ours is still a classless society. However misguided the vision of a classless society is, often embedded inside this notion is the positive understanding that wealth can be shared, that class hierarchy predicated on the assumption that those who have the most materially should rule over the rest need not exist.

Sadly, the grave injustices created by contemporary transnational white supremacist capitalist patriarchy, this ever-widening gap between the rich and the poor, has been the catalyst compelling folks who are economically privileged to consider their class, to think about what they do with money. Many individuals who have economic privilege do not want to use money or reproduce material excess in ways that require the oppression, exploitation, and dehumanization of their fellow citizens. While few of these individuals are rich (it is difficult to create and reproduce wealth without exploiting others), a vast majority have class privilege that provides them/us (I include myself in this category) with any resources to share.

Those among us who are progressive, who are democratic socialists, know that wealth can be redistributed in ways that challenge and change class exploitation and oppression. As individuals we promote and perpetuate this process of redistribution by both unorganized and organized sharing and giving of resources. In the book *Robin Hood*

Was Right: A Guide to Giving Your Money for Social Change, authors Joan Garner, Chuck Collins, and Pam Rogers state in their preface: "Tipping the balance of resources to include more of humanity is an adventurous, thrilling, and worthwhile pursuit. Charity is good, but supporting and creating social change are about power. Power can infuse lives with purpose and dignity. That opens up the possibility of joy. The life of the giver, as well as that of receiver, is transformed." Folks who are not rich give a greater portion of their resources to those who stand in need than those who have great wealth, who may also give but in ways that reinforce their ruling class power. Their giving is not aimed at redistributing wealth or eliminating class hierarchy.

Large numbers of progressive folks with economic privilege genuinely oppose class exploitation and oppression and actively work to challenge and change class elitism. Our activism is not collectively organized under any one rubric so it often is easy for mainstream status quo culture to pretend that we and our activism do not exist. Many folks with economic privilege, whether progressive or not, have begun to critically question consumer capitalism, both the ethic of greed it encourages and the obsession with getting that it rewards. Across race, class, gender, and sexual practice individuals share the obsession with getting. Working in the public school systems, sharing and teaching about justice, I find that the one common yearning children share, whether they are in fancy private schools with small classrooms or huge overcrowded institutions, is the longing to be wealthy. Already they identify with ruling class values, already they are obsessed with getting. No wonder children are viewed as the new consumers, the new market, and by the end of the year 2000 they will have spent more than five hundred billion dollars. These children, like their adult peers, do not link their longing for wealth with uncritical acceptance and support of transnational white supremacist capitalist patriarchy. They simply believe they are longing for the "good life" and that this life has to be bought.

Increasingly, though, we hear from individual voices that dare to share that economic privilege does not necessarily bring the good life. In many self-help and new age books, folks with privilege are encouraged to be mindful about their relationship to money. Books like *Your Money or Your Life,* by Joe Dominguez and Vicki Robin, remind us of the human costs to pursuing great wealth. Many of the young folks who have acquired great wealth before the age of forty as a result of their work in the field of new technologies willingly testify that they work long hours to make, sustain, and reproduce this wealth. And like those who have acquired wealth or excessive economic privilege before them, they often find when they make time for something other than work that the space is empty, or the culture of getting is all they know, so they make their personal life an extension of their economic life.

In *Let's Develop,* social therapist Fred Newman calls attention to the reality that the culture of getting often leads most of us to be "deprived, emotionally disadvantaged, and underdeveloped." He makes the observation that getting is not necessarily immoral but that "it's simply that, like cholesterol, in many life situations getting isn't very good for our emotional health." The only way to counter the culture of getting is to give. Significantly, Newman shares this powerful insight: "Everyday sexism, racism and the other isms are as much the products of the culture of getting as they are expressions of the way the economy and politics are organized. In the absence of creating a new emotional culture, there doesn't seem to be much hope of doing a lot about them." Indeed, concern for their emotional well-being, concern about everyday racism, sexism, and homophobia are often the issues that lead individuals to question the politics of class, to interrogate their relationship to capitalism, to money, to giving. It is no accident that outspoken critiques of race and gender inequities are often silent about class. For class touches us all in the place where we live, whether we are economically advantaged or disadvantaged. Folks without privilege, who are yearning to have, do not want to be critical of class elitism, and folks with privilege, who want to maintain it at the expense of others, are careful not to talk about ending class hierarchies.

When I use the rubric of transnational white supremacist capitalist patriarchy as the standard by which I measure my own engagement with systems of domination, it is always the politics of class that calls out the deepest challenge. In the space of race and gender I am most likely to stand among those victimized; class is the one place where I have a choice about where I stand. Many folks with economic privilege who remain silent about economic injustice are silent because they do not want to interrogate where they stand. Sadly, all too often they stand in a place that is hypocritical. To challenge racism or sexism or both without linking these systems to economic structures of exploitation and our collective participation in the upholding and maintenance of such structures, however marginal that engagement may be, is ultimately to betray a vision of justice for all. Such hypocrisy has been displayed blatantly by Western feminists from privileged classes (most of whom are white) who deplore sexist mistreatment of women by men, while condoning paying women of color both here and abroad inadequate wages (often to perform the labor that "frees" the privileged to be liberated career women) or supporting the elimination of welfare. The transnational corporate capitalist agenda is gendered and racialized.

All too often the freedom that Western women prize is won at the price of the enslavement of women elsewhere. To deny this fact is to deny the link between global capital and the local capitalist regime which governs our lives. When we remember that women are half of the human race, the poorest citizens on the planet performing approximately two-thirds of the world's work and earning about one tenth of the world's income and less than one-hundredth of its property, we face more directly the interconnectedness of race, class, and gender. Early on in feminist movement, revolutionary feminist thinkers critiqued the reformist notion that economic power was synonymous with freedom.

In *Feminist Theory: From Margin to Center,* I challenged the assumption that paid work would liberate women, calling attention to the fact that when bourgeois white women talked about work as liberating they meant careers. In recent years many of these economically privileged women have abandoned competitive careerism because it did not "liberate" them or enable them to have a balance. Like well-off men they found themselves placing work above all else. When we work too much and are bereft of meaningful time, we overcompensate by spending. This is why children and teenagers are the new consumers; they are given economic rewards in place of genuine engagement and connection by parents who are not fully emotionally developed and who lack time.

In her most recent work, feminist thinker Julie Matthaei champions feminist critique of competitive careering. Her essay "Healing Ourselves, Healing Our Economy: Paid Work, Unpaid Work, and the Next Stage of Feminist Economic Transformation" chronicles the shift in feminist thinking about labor. She finds it hopeful that women are bringing a relational ethics of care into the public sphere—one that calls for socially responsible consumption and investment: "These movements urge people to use their purchasing power and investment dollars to pressure firms to be socially responsible—by supporting firms that are 'green' (environmentally friendly), family friendly and feminist and anti-racist, uninvolved in military, cigarette or alcohol production, worker-owned, etc. These movements organize consumers and investors to choose on criteria other than simple cost minimization/profit maximization thus supporting the movement for socially responsible entrepreneurship." Matthaei sees these choices as supporting our "true self-interest in a safe, sustainable, healthy, and just economy and society."

In order to end oppressive class hierarchy we must think against the grain. Resisting unnecessary consumerism, living simply, and abundantly sharing resources are the easiest ways to begin an economic shift that will ultimately create balance. Job sharing where a living wage is paid to everyone is another crucial way to address both unemployment and the need to provide parents, female and male, more time to create positive home environments where they can parent effectively. Working to create electoral politics wherein as citizens we can vote for where we want our tax dollars to go, for education or military spending, for aid to the poor and disenfranchised or military spending. Many citizens of this nation would welcome the opportunity to pay their tax dollars for institutional services that redistribute wealth. Our interdependency and care for neighbors and strangers could be highlighted by programs that would allow those with materially plenty to economically support families in need and deduct this money from taxes. Ironically, one can deduct money sent to the poor in other countries but not if we give to those who are desperately needy where we live.

The need for safe affordable housing will be the economic issue that will soon galvanize the American public as the middle-class and lower-middle-class folks increasingly find themselves economically displaced and without access to shelter. Hopefully, they will join with the disenfranchised poor, the homeless, to demand affordable housing. Perhaps the progressive rich will consider buying land and creating not just affordable housing but positive diverse communities that are founded on democratic principles that promote the well-being of everyone. Until such communities abound we will have no evidence to prove that communalism works, that localized democratic government that coexists with the state can improve lives. The time to join together and reimagine our economic futures is now. The time to rethink class, to find out where we stand is now.

I began this book expressing my fear that I did not know enough hard-core economic jargon to talk meaningfully about class. However, my silence, like all our silences about class, easily becomes part of the collusion, part of our acquiescence and participation in unjust economic practices, an unwitting support of class elitism. Most folks I meet in life, and I meet thousands of strangers while lecturing around the nation, want to cross the boundaries of class to know folks with diverse class experiences. It is this longing that will inspire us to find the ways to end exploitative and oppressive class hierarchies. As I have confessed, crossing class boundaries is no simple journey, even when we are among family and kin who have diverse class backgrounds.

I am thankful to have been raised in this nation by poor rural grandparents who farmed, who were in many ways self-sufficient, by parents who were working class and proud of their capacity to work hard and well. They taught me to honor labor, whether paid or unpaid, to love the poor, to learn from them for all they have to teach us about survival. They taught me that to be poor was no cause for shame, that one's dignity and integrity of being could never be determined by money, by market values. To love the poor among us, to acknowledge their essential goodness and humanity is a mighty challenge to class hierarchy. Had my grandparents—sharecroppers and farmers—and my parents—maids and janitors—not taught me to look past class, to look past the trappings of money to see the inner self, I might never have learned to value myself and others rightfully. For this shared wisdom, borne of their experiences of enslavement, of indentured servitude, of hard labor in the white supremacist capitalist patriarchal south, has helped me not only to know where I stand but to stand firm.

My class allegiance and solidarity will always be with working people, folk of all classes, who see money as useful insomuch as it enhances our well-being. The time will come when wealth will be redistributed, when the workers of the world will once again unite— standing for economic justice—for a world where we can all have enough to live fully and well.

where we stand:
CLASS MATTERS

bell hooks

Laura L. Miller